Time Space and Designs for Actors

Maxine Klein
Boston University

*format conceived by
Cynthia Gregg Whitham*

Houghton Mifflin Company

Boston

Atlanta

Dallas

Geneva, Illinois

Hopewell, New Jersey

Palo Alto

London

Library of Congress Catalog Card Number: 74–15397

ISBN: 0-395-18612-9

Excerpt from *Joe Egg* by Peter Nichols: Reprinted by permission of Grove Press, Inc. Copyright © 1967 by Peter Nichols.

"My life closed twice before its close," by Emily Dickinson: Reprinted by permission of the publishers and the Trustees of Amherst College from Thomas H. Johnson, Editor, *The Poems of Emily Dickinson*, Cambridge, Mass.: The Belknap Press of Harvard University Press, Copyright, 1951, 1955, by The President and Fellows of Harvard College.

Excerpt from *Yerma* by Federico Garcia Lorca: Federico Garcia Lorca, *Three Tragedies*, translated by James Graham Luhan and Richard O'Connell. Copyright 1947, 1955 by New Directions Publishing Corporation. Reprinted by permission of New Directions Publishing Corporation.

Excerpt from *Summer and Smoke* by Tennessee Williams: *The Theatre of Tennessee Williams*, Vol. II. Copyright 1948 by Tennessee Williams. Reprinted by permission of New Directions Publishing Corporation.

Excerpt from *No Exit* by Jean-Paul Sartre: Reprinted from *No Exit and The Flies*, by Jean-Paul Sartre, translated by Stuart Gilbert, copyright 1946, by permission of Alfred A. Knopf, Inc.

Photos by Erik Hansen

I would like to thank

all the teachers of acting who have preceded me

but more importantly

all the students of acting who have accompanied me

Contents

v

4. Body Acting Centers 53

x

Foreword

This handbook for actors is designed to cultivate the actor's sense of self

    to increase his imaginative
              creative
                    technical abilities

        to release his energy resources.

For too long American acting,
weighed down by an almost exclusive reliance on the Method,
has had about it a slowness, a heaviness, a lack of vigor.
It has been as if American actors were moving in slow motion, under water.

The extraordinary thrust of American energy
everywhere in evidence in the streets, on campuses, in jazz and rock,
in the very movement of contemporary life, was seldom on the stage—
at least not on the establishment stage.

Here life methodically slowed down, turned in upon itself, and waited.

Not that the Method is without merit.
Its emphasis is on truth, on making everything the actor does on stage
believeable to himself and, therefore, to the audience.

That emphasis on truth is the very essence of stage life.
Without it, nothing the actor does on stage has worth:
if the actor is not truthful,
s/he cannot create a character in whom the audience can believe.
And if the audience does not believe the actor,
what matters his pacing
    prating and
    posturing?

The limitation of the Method,
at least the limitation in the way some have interpreted it,
does not lie in its insistence that the actor be truthful
so that s/he can create a viable reality for himself.
The Method's limitation lies rather in the reality it asks the actor to create.

The reality of the Method has been the reality of the small moment
                    the small passion.
It has been the sentimental reality of the working man next door and
                    the lonely woman upstairs.

It has not been the reality of extraordinary energy
extreme passion
high-intensity living.

The Method, in effect, has dealt most effectively with
the mundane, the low key,
reducing the subjects it treats to that ordinary level.

By default, it has failed with the bizarre
spectacular
extraordinary
magnificent.

This means it has failed to discover those bizarre
spectacular
extraordinary
magnificent qualities in all of us.

This handbook is designed to help you, the actor, rediscover your possibilities.
Not that in doing so you will be asked to go against the grain of the Method.
Quite the contrary.
Like the Method this handbook will ask
that everything you do have its basis in belief.
It will ask you to begin where the Method begins, but
it will challenge you to go far beyond where the Method ends.

A word about the title *Time, Space, and Designs.*
It is meant to describe the work you will be asked to do with this book
in as concrete a way as possible.

T   This handbook suggests ways for you to become an actor,
not only in the classroom and on stage
but in the time you spend off stage.
The notion underlying this round-the-clock concept is that all artists,
whether they are painters, novelists, or what-have-you,
use the world around them as raw material
          stimuli
            workshop.

M To the end of making the world your acting workshop,
there are carrythrough sections in each chapter
detailing ways you can use what you do in your everyday life to perfect your craft.
The assumption is that you can discover
         grow
          learn

E   in this round-the-clock life/art crisscross.

S   This handbook is spaced on the page
P   in such a way as to pull you
A   into the creative processes you will experience.
C   The spacing is not sentence/paragraph dictated
E   but experience prompted.

D   The handbook is composed of designs.
E   These are concrete, realizable acting situations
S   so structured
I   so designed
G   that through experiencing them you learn acting principles
N   transferable to virtually all acting situations.

Because this is a handbook of designs
you will not memorize rules of acting;
you will not study *how* to act.

YOU WILL ACT.

You will learn by doing.
To this end, each acting experience is divided into four parts,
three of them experiential:

a brief explanation of the acting *principles*
to be experienced in the design

a body-spirit *preparation*

the *design* itself
to be performed in class with fellow actors and a teacher-guide

a *carrythrough*
suggesting ways for you to practice the acting principles
in the solitude of your own home and
in the public process of everyday life.

Now
with the handbook,
with the aid of a teacher-guide-evaluator, and
through your life in and out of the classroom

begin your gradual development as an actor.

To be sure,
by the time you have experienced the last design in this handbook,

you will not be a full-fledged actor:
you will be quite aware that acting,
like all art,
is a lifelong, long-lived process.

But even though you will not be an accomplished artisan,
you will be well along the journeyman route.

For through *experience*

you will have absorbed and assimilated principles of acting

you will have begun to develop a reliable consciousness of what good acting is

you will have developed an organic way to practice your craft

not only in the specific event of preparing for and
putting on a play in a theatre,
but also in the private process of working by yourself
in the public process of living in the workaday world.

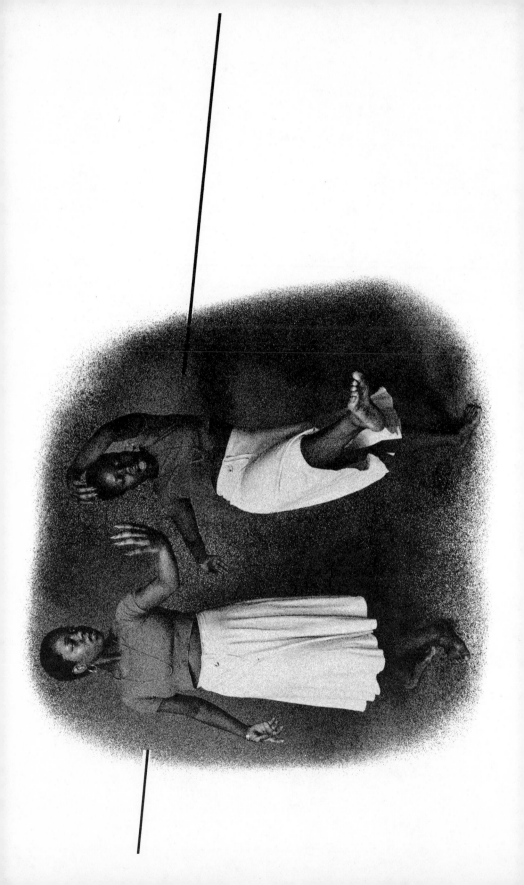

1 The Actor in Space

Actors must assert their right to s p a c e .

They must claim it
        fill   it
        make it $v_ib_ra_te$ with their presence.

No time now for modesty
                hiding
                self-effacement.

4

From the time they enter stage space until they leave it,
actors must give out energy charges that say:

"It is all right to look at me.
I have trained for and earned my right to this space.
I will be interesting enough and do interesting enough things
to merit attention."

Preparation: Body commanding space

Close your eyes.

See your spinal column before you,
one vertebra stacked on the other in a long, straight, strong line.
Once you have seen the vertebral column in your mind's eye,

Assume a sufficiently wide stance
so that you have solid support in your legs and feet.

Bend over from your waist,
letting your arms and neck and head hang loosely.

Bend your knees a bit
so that you do not unnecessarily tense them.
Hang there over yourself for a time, relaxed and easy.
In this position,

Say, "Ha, ha, ha."
Let the words fall out of your mouth,
splashing softly on the floor.
Allow the air passing over your vocal chords to warm them up,
getting them ready for stage use.

Notice as you say these words the total lack of strain in your neck,
an area you frequently and uselessly tense up when you speak.
In this bent-over position it is almost impossible
to put strain on your neck and vocal chords;
your neck is hanging loose and relaxed,
allowing your voice to come naturally from the diaphragm,
unimpeded by any strain that tense neck muscles
might otherwise force on it.

Continue to produce the ha ha ha sounds for two or three minutes
until your vocal chords are warm and limber,
ready to go to work.

Soon you will rise to an upright position, but when you do, bear
in mind that just as you produced sound without tensing your
neck when you were hanging over yourself, you must continue
to produce sounds without tensing when you are standing
upright.

Begin to rise
by stacking your vertebrae one on top of the other
                              one on top of the other

until all are aligned in a straight, strong column.
Begin this stacking action at the base of your spine and
continue one by one through the vertebrae until the neck vertebrae,
the last to be aligned because they are located at the top,
are in a line with those of your spine.

Stand still for a moment and focus your attention
on the vertebral column that is supporting you
and giving you strength. In your mind's eye,
see that column, long and straight,
supplying the support the rest of your body needs
to move freely through space.

Design: Body commanding space

Once you feel your support in your spine,
let the rest of your body relax.

Focus your attention directly in front of you.

Feel yourself poised in air.

Command the circle of space around you.

You are the center, the giver of energy.
The power you have is not hostile, but easy, personal power,
allowing you to enjoy the space and yourself in the space.

Stop.
Check to see that your bottom is tucked in,
not urging out, making you sway back.
See that your weight is on your toes,
not your heels, putting you off balance.
Feel your body's strength and support in your spine.
Let your arms and shoulders be free, totally relaxed.

Feel once again the space around you vibrate with your energy.
The energy emanates from your center and charges the space.

Begin to move.

Notice the other class members moving around you.
Let their energy and life inform you,
giving you greater energy, greater life.

Feel the air part in front of you.
Cut your way through space.

7

Use strong strides, claiming the floor beneath you
as much as the space around you.

Move fast.
Move slow.
But always *move charged with energy.*

Now add to your movement whirls
                              turns
                                  stops.

Start off in one direction
turn on a dime and go in another
whirl in space
move quickly, then
stop suddenly
poised
controlled
full of energy.

Move again,
all the while enjoying yourself and all the others in space.
Flash about like a young, imperious lion.

At this point start to play off the other members of the class.
When you encounter one another,
STOP.
Form dynamic, meaningful relationships with your bodies.

Move again.
This time when you meet give out whooping sounds of delight.
The whoops can change to "Hi" and "Hello," but
it is essential that they remain huge energy sounds.
Let the strength and good spirits of everyone else inform you
so that your energy naturally increases.
You will be supported by everyone else's energy flow
just as your energy flow will support them.

Stop to check yourself:
Bend over from your waist
as you did in the warming-up exercise.
Produce the ha ha ha sounds for a time;
then make big whooping sounds.
After you have charged the space around you with big sounds,
without straining your neck,
gradually rise by stacking your vertebrae
one on top of the other until all are aligned.
Continue to make big, whooping sounds as you rise,
making certain that you do not at any time
tense your neck muscles.

10

Once again, begin to move through space.

Encounter one another.

Form dynamic relationships with your bodies.

Whoop out a greeting.

Make the space around you vibrate *with your presence.*

Carrythrough

Let your body command the space of your own home.

Reread the instructions for the design.
Don't just pass your eyes over them like a computer scanner.
ASSIMILATE.

Recall any comments made about your movement by the teacher-guide.

Do the design.

In the privacy of your own home
you might also want to try this design unclothed.

Free
in its natural state

unencumbered by clothing,
let your body command space.

You are so at one with your body that
you feel no embarrassment at your nakedness.

You should also try the design with music,
letting the varying rhythms and tempos infuse your body
                                      inform your movement.

Let the music support you
                 put you at ease with yourself.

Do the design in public.

Every time you walk somewhere
incorporate what you have learned from this experience:

Align your spine.

Feel yourself poised in air.

Command the space around you.

Walk forward using strong strides.

Enjoy yourself in space.

2. Your Body, Your Self

BODY RELEASE

The actor's body is her/his instrument.

In McLuhan terms, the *medium* of the actor's body is her/his acting *message*.

Thus you, the actor, must know your body—as well as a dancer or an athlete knows her/his body *(maybe even better)*.

13

14

You must know how to relax your body
            how to turn it on and off
            how to move it
            how to allow it to stand in stillness and repose
            how to express yourself through it.

For only with this knowledge
and the power
        stamina
        flexibility
        expressiveness
that this knowledge brings
will you have the organic command you need for your creative and
                                    performance work.

Preparation: Body relaxation

Study yourself in a mirror,
or if there are no mirrors, work in pairs.

Examine one another's bodies
both in stillness and in movement.

Discover one another's tension areas.

    Is one arm held tightly?
    Is the neck jutting forward?

Is the jaw clenched?
Is there a lack of flexibility in the legs?

Once you have discovered where you put tension,
you are ready to learn how to take that tension away.

You are ready to relax.

Design: Relaxing through tension and release

Imagine that you are about to tighten yourself into a tiny knot.
Now count to fifteen slowly,
tensing your body into a tinier and tinier knot as you count.

When you reach fifteen, maintain that extreme tension for a moment.

Now start to relax, slowly, again to a count of fifteen.
Once you are totally relaxed, maintain that repose for a time.

You may repeat this design a couple of times until
you are physically aware of total body relaxation.

Once you have experienced body relaxation through physical exercise,
you are ready to relax through mental volition.

Design: Relaxing through volition

Lie down in space.

Close your eyes.

Direct your attention to your feet,
first to one foot ⎤ and release all tension.
then the other ⎦

This will not involve a physical adjustment. Your mind alone
can release the tension. The proof of the pudding will be that
with this mind-willed release, you will feel your toes and the
balls of your feet begin to tingle as your blood, no longer
constricted by unnecessary tension, flows more freely.

Direct your attention to your legs.
One at a time take away tension from them.
Let them become **heavy** and sink to the floor.
They become so heavy that should you get up
you would leave an imprint on the floor!

Throughout this design
let all the sounds you hear in the room and beyond
take you deeper and deeper into relaxation.
In this state you will not feel sleepy;

on the contrary, you will discover more energy flow
since no tension will be there to constrict it.

Continue in this same easy but concentrated way
through the rest of your body,
directing your attention-to-relax

now to your intestines

now to your stomach

now to your lungs

    to your hands
        arms
           shoulders
              neck

    to your spinal column

to each and every part of your face from your lips and
                            tongue and on up

to the hairs on the top of your head.

18

Once you have relaxed and released all parts of your body,
from the balls of your feet to the hairs on your scalp

you are ready to *float.*

Lying in perfect repose,
let your legs extend until they touch the wall.

_____

Trust your imagination.
It can take you inside yourself
            outside yourself
                anywhere you want to go.

Feel the texture of the wall with your feet.
Now let your torso and neck extend
until your head touches the opposite wall.
Feel the wall with your scalp.

Extend your left arm and hand.
Touch, *feel*, the wall on your left.
Do the same with your right arm and hand.

You are now floating, perfectly suspended in air.

As you float between the four walls of the room,
enjoy the sensation
and enjoy the power of your imagination
to take you anywhere you want to go,
allow you to do anything you want to do.

Be assured also that when you are on stage
and feel a part of your body tensing
you can direct your attention to it and release tension.

Your mind put the tension there and
your mind can take it away!

Carrythrough

Look at other people on the street, in stores, wherever.
Notice their tension.
See the crippling effect it has on their bodies.
Become vigilant in warding off tension from your own body.

When you are about to go to sleep at night
direct your attention to all parts of your body.
One at a time, release the tension from each part.

Relax.
Deeply.
More deeply.
Sleep.

Wake up refreshed.
Ready to work.

Direct your attention—at any time of the day or night—to your body. Examine it closely to discover if you have unwittingly tensed up any part. Then direct your attention to the part where tension exists—say your shoulders or your legs—and take the tension away, allowing your body to assume its natural flexibility and control.

BODY INSIDE, BODY OUTSIDE

Ralph Waldo Emerson once said that
we are all artists more than we know—
artists in our eyes
in our ears
in our everything.

In the process of growing up, however,
most of us have had our artist obscured.
In "maturing" we have lost the artist of our body.
We have lost the sense of joy in ourselves.

Notice how a baby can find almost infinite delight in h$_{is}^{er}$ toes.
We adults forget we have toes unless they hurt us from too-tight shoes.
How dreadful to think about our body only when it is in pain or need!

As actors

as people

we must regain touch with our bodies.

We must recognize them for what they are—our SELVES.

If we neglect
    overlook
        become dissociated from our bodies
we become dissociated from our selves.

One reason we have become dissociated from our bodies is
that we don't know our bodies.

21

Think about it.
We devote great time to knowing books, other people, food, and language, but we devote almost no time to knowing the important part of ourself that is our body.

Time now to know our bodies. Our selves.

Preparation: Body trip

In the following design you are going to enter your body through your imagination in order to see and experience all parts of your body from the inside.

Don't be concerned that you are not literally, scientifically, medically aware of how your body looks from the inside. Let your imagination help you out here. In other words, see your bodily parts not as a doctor or scientist would see them but as you would see them.

In other words
don't see charts, lines, cells.

See   **colors**
       shapes
       motion

Feel texture
pulse
electricity

Taste salt
sour
sweet

Hear squeaks
thuds
gurgles

Smell natural smells:
sweat
blood
fat

Disregard the commercials; they're good smells.

Design: Body trip

Lie down on the floor.
Close your eyes.
Make yourself very, very, very tiny.

Now enter your body through an orifice—an ear
                                              an eye
                                              your nose
                                              your mouth
                                              your genitals.

Once inside,
slowly begin to explore and experience all parts of your body.
Pay particular attention to the parts of your body
where you have experienced difficulty.

If your stomach frequently ties itself in knots,
examine minutely your stomach.

If you frequently experience backaches,
go to the part of your back where you have difficulty
and explore it very carefully.

Do not, however, let this be solely a therapeutic trip.
Allow yourself to spend time in the places
you experience great bodily pleasure.
You've been puritanical long enough about your body.

Be a hedonist!

If you enjoy certain smells,
go into your nose and
see how it responds to and relays sensory orders.

If you enjoy eating,
follow a bite of cherry cheesecake from your mouth
down through the rest of your body.

Throughout this trip take t i m e . . .
You will need an hour or two for your first exposure to this
dimension of yourself and you should plan on returning.
Do not be satisfied until you have truly experienced all
parts of your body.

Find out how each part of your body looks
                                        feels
                                        smells
                                        works
                                        plays.

As you explore, keep your eyes closed,
but move and make sounds if you wish.
Throughout this odyssey, maintain the attitude of an explorer.
The only difference between you and Columbus is that
he went to a country for new experiences, riches, and insights
and you are going inside *your self.*

25

When you have finished your maiden voyage, swim to an exit and come out.

Carrythrough

If you repeatedly have a problem with some part of your body, set time aside for a body trip.

If you experience shortness of breath
every time you perform in front of people,
set aside some time to go into your diaphragm
lungs
throat.

See how beautifully the lungs and diaphragm work.
Now see how tensing your neck muscles ⎤ constrict the flow
holding your breath ⎬ of air and sound.
shallow breathing ⎦

To supplement any of these imaginary trips you could profit immensely by reading as much *scientific-medical* material as you can about the body. Problems have a way of ceasing, or at least diminishing substantially, once you understand the situation in which they arise. Once you

have studied the problem, take a body trip and experience
subjectively what you have read objectively.

Of equal importance to learning about your body through science is
learning about it through *art*.
Go to museums,
not to be bored, to rush through, to tell someone else you have been there.

This time go to *experience* bodies as seen and exalted by artists.

Don't try to see everything at once.
Zero in on no more than two or three sculptures
                        two or three paintings of the human body.

Give yourself time to delight in
each artist's delight in the form
                        texture
                        rhythm
                        grace   of the human body.

It takes only a moment to transfer that delight to your own body,
but the results can last forever.

Through the scientific-artistic assimilative process,
you will get in touch with yourself and
reawaken in yourself the artist Emerson talked about.

27

3. INTENTIONS

On stage—as off—people communicate as much through the way they say words as through the words themselves.

Whole worlds of meaning are communicated behind
{ below, above, during, after } words.

These levels of meaning are communicated through

the energy of the character's thought

the intensity of h^{er}_{is} feeling

the sound of h^{er}_{is} voice

the rhythm of h^{er}_{is} movement

h^{er}_{is} acts

and perhaps most important of all, through

h^{er}_{is} *intention.*

An intention is an extension of what the word implies:
it intends to create a state of feeling
in the character to whom it is played
so that the character will *feel* and *act* in the desired way.

If, in a scene between Alice and Bill,
Alice's intention is to make Bill feel happy
so that he will seek out her company again in the future,

then the way Alice thinks
talks
looks—

everything she does while she is playing her intention—
should be a direct result of it.

Intention ——————→ *Emotion* ——→ *Act*

Alice   Bill   so that
intends to make   feel happy   he will seek out her company again.

Clearly, most of the actor's modes of expression are dictated
by intentions. Yet as important as the intentions that inform
words and actions are, all too often actors rely on words alone
to convey meaning. They decide in some arbitrary pact with a
standard dictionary that if they, themselves, first understand
the words in a denotative sense and then say the words as
clearly, as loudly, and—in the old school of acting—as
beautifully as possible, they need do no more.
They will have delivered and
the audience will have received
everything that is essential from that dramatic moment.

In a scene David is to say "I love you" to Alfre.
David says the words, perhaps with all due sincerity and intensity,
but he forgets to pinpoint his intention in saying these three potent words
and the phrase falls flat.

31

What could his intention be when he says, "I love you"?
Almost anything in the world.

David might be sorry that he loves Alfre and
try to make her equally as sorry
so that she will leave him.

He might try to threaten her
so that she will stay.

He might try to disarm her
so that she will tell the truth.

He might try to convince her that he is telling the truth
(though he is lying)
so that she will give him money.

He might want to relax her
so that he can seduce her.

And on and on.
The possibilities are limitless.

The point is
that every time an actor speaks on stage s/he must know
what s/he wants to make the other character feel and do.

Moreover
s/he must remember that in stage life
a character's intention is frequently not the literal meaning
of the words s/he is saying:

At a party Louise says, "Oh, what a beautiful dress!" to Ann.
But Louise does not really like the dress at all.
She is embarrassed by Ann's choice of clothing and
is trying to hide her embarrassment in an easy compliment.

At work an employee says to his boss who asks him to work overtime,
"Yes, sir. Glad to do it."
The fact of the matter is he hates doing extra work and
he hates his boss for asking him.
His intention is to be overly civil in order to conceal his hatred,
thus convincing his boss that he is the ideal employee.

Because your intention is equally as significant as
the literal meaning of the words you are saying,
you, the actor, must always
determine your intention before you speak.

And it is safe for you to assume that your intention
as often as not will be at odds with
the literal meaning of the words you are saying.

33

72097

Preparation: Realizing intentions

The following designs need an extensive physical and vocal warm-up.

For three minutes
hang over from your waist and repeat, "Ha, ha, ha"
as you rise
vertebra by vertebra
to an upright position.

Then
say, "Hey yo yo yo la la la ma ma ma" over and over again.
Say the phrase to the person next to you
       the person across the room
       the person in the next state
       the person in the next country.

Design: Realizing intentions through gibberish

Stand alone in space

Close your eyes

See in your mind's eye
a person you love or have loved.

Think the words "I love you"
and consider the multitudes of things you might try to accomplish
through these words at the moment you are saying them to the loved one.

Are you trying to make h$^{er}_{im}$ responsible for you
so s/he won't leave you?

Are you trying to placate h$^{er}_{im}$
so that s/he won't explode in anger?

Are you teasing h$^{er}_{im}$
so s/he will join you in your playful mood?

Are you hoping to divert h$^{er}_{im}$
so s/he won't remember to phone someone?

Once you have chosen your intention
see the other in your mind's eye and
say "I love you" to h$^{er}_{im}$,
but don't use the words themselves.
Use gibberish.

Think: "I am an hour late for our appointment.
I'll divert h$^{er}_{im}$ so s/he won't be angry."

Now think the words "I love you,"
but say them through the medium of other sounds and vocal tones.

You may purr;
you may say, "Ta ta ta;"
you may choose any sound to realize the words "I love you"
with your particular intention of diverting the other
so s/he won't explode into anger.

After you have explored one intention,
proceed to another.
You may change the mental image of the person to whom you are speaking
as often as you wish.

Design: Realizing intentions through gibberish and movement

Find a partner.

One of you will be the activator,
the other the activated.

The activator will decide on a particular intention:

s/he wants the other to feel depressed or
fearful or
busily happy.

The activator will then provide the sound/feeling/movement intention for the other's emotional state.
The activated is to react emotionally and physically to the activator's intention.

The activator's intention might be to intimidate the other so s/he will crouch in fear or run away.

The activator could assume a sadistic tone of command and make sharp rat-tat-tat sounds interspersed with foot stamps and hand claps, all aggressively directed toward making the other feel submissive and tense.

The activated might then respond like a tiny squirrel of a person, futilely relying on quick evasive movements to protect him_{er}self from the activator's attacks.

The activator can quickly change h_{is}^{er} intention and sound, transforming from this sadistic monster into a sweet, loving protector whose intention is to make the other feel warm and loved so s/he will play.

In this new persona the activator could make soft cooing sounds and gently pat the other's hand.

37

The activated would respond accordingly,
perhaps by lying on the floor in an open, trusting way,
perhaps by skipping about playfully
like a favored child warm in parental love,
perhaps by performing tricks in order to gain even more approval
from the activator-admirer.

The activator can do anything s/he feels.
The point is that
whatever the activated feels and does
will be a direct result of the activator's intention.

Of course, neither the sound nor the movement in this design
need be realistic or specifically human.

The activator can bark and nudge the other with h$^{er}_{is}$ nose, and
the activated can romp about on all fours like a playful puppy;
the activator can make soft, undulating movements
and emit airy, easy sounds
to which the activated might respond by
becoming like a flower opening to the sun.

There are hundreds of choices available to both the activator
and the activated. The point here is to experiment in a truthful,
sentient, open way with as many possibilities as you have time

and imagination for. In so doing, teach yourself the innumerable levels of communicative power available to you through playing intentions.

Teach yourself, in effect, to what an extraordinary degree truthful intention energy communicates.

After one person has played the activator for a while, the partners should change roles. Before resuming the action, it might be worthwhile for each of you to discuss some of the things you felt about the experience.
After this period of constructive criticism, resume,
each in your new role.

In the beginning the two of you will continue this way, consciously deciding to alternate roles. But after you have worked together for a while, you will discover that you can change back and forth from activator to activated as easily and naturally as if the two of you were one organism. In this symbiotic state there will scarcely be a beat between the intention-input and the physicalized emotional response.

Guides for the activator:

Vary your matter of expressing intentions—tones
                                        rhythms
                                            body positions—

so that the person you are acting on
is prompted to vary the modes of his. responses.

Know and *think* and *feel* what you are doing.
Don't be a disembodied voice trying to excite your partner
to states of feeling and action.
It won't work.
If you are truly honest you will soon discover that
the other will develop a total characterization and action
based only on your communicated intentions.

Guides for the activated:

Keep yourself open to the moment.
Don't put barriers between yourself and the motivation.
Respond fully and immediately,
as you do in life.

Allow your acting instrument to be so totally pliant that
you experience and
    physicalize all the nuances of the emotional input.

Don't just respond with your arms and legs.
Feel and move from your own power center,
charging your whole being with energy.

Design: Realizing intentions through movement and words, in situation

Accepting the definition that an actor's intention is
to make the other character feel a certain emotion
so that the other will act in a particular way,
use one phrase to realize five different intentions.

To realize fully each of five intentions through this phrase,
create in great detail
each situation in which you will use the phrase.

You must know who you are
   where you are
   who the other character is in relation to you
   what you want to make the other feel.

A possible phrase is "I'm home, Julie."
A possible situation is:

You are an errant husband.
It is three o'clock in the morning.
Your wife, you hope, is sleeping.

You want to sneak into the apartment
without waking her up; yet
should she be awake or should you awaken her,
you want her to think everything is quite
ordinary so she won't get up and confront you.
You decide to act so innocent that
should she get up she would believe
you thought it no later than midnight.
You open the door to your apartment and
say in as tiny but confidently innocent
a voice as possible."I'm home, Julie."

Now use the same phrase in the four other situations.
In each situation
(as in every situation on stage in a play)
know who you are
    where you are
    who the other person is in relation to you
    what you want the other person to feel and then do
when you say the phrase.

In figuring out each intention it is best to word it as an infinitive and
                                                    a ''so'' clause:

I want the other to cry
    so s/he will free h^{er}imself emotionally

    to laugh
    so s/he will forget h^{er}is hurt

    to feel I'm right
    so s/he will forgive me

    to fear me
    so s/he will study harder

    to think everything is O.K.
    so s/he will not worry.

When you act the words in situation,
make certain you use every communicative resource
appropriate to the realization of your intention.
Speak with your entire body
                mind
                  spirit.

Continue this design
substituting other phrases and
creating other situations.

Design: Realizing intentions through movement alone

Once again know who you are
where you are
who the other character is in relation to you
what you want to make the other feel.

Now walk into a room where the other is.
By your walk
⎰ energy
⎱ tone ⎱ your intention
mood
will

make the other feel what you want h$^{er}_{im}$ to feel and
do what you want h$^{er}_{im}$ to do.

Walk in a rejected way
barely look at h$^{er}_{im}$
sit down facing away   so s/he will come over to comfort you.

Leap and bound into the room
do a wild dance around h$^{er}_{im}$ so h$^{er}_{is}$ spirits will be lifted and
s/he will laugh and
dance with you.

___ Communicate these intentions truthfully and you will be surprised at how much you can say to someone with your body intention alone.

Carrythrough

When you walk into a restaurant, a department store, or any public service place and are approached by a salesperson, notice how h$^{er}_{is}$ intention affects you as much if not more than h$^{er}_{is}$ words.

S/he may say, "Can I help you?" but h$^{er}_{is}$ intention is to make you feel that helping you is the last thing in the world s/he wants to do. S/he wants you to eat quickly, get out soon, and in the meantime bother h$^{er}_{im}$ as little as possible.

Tune into how people say your name.
Discover their intention.

You arrive home.
You take off your coat.
All your mother has to say is your first name and you know precisely what she wants you to feel and do!

The intention played in that one word can make you tense with anticipation
make you angry
all but reduce you to tears or
make you break out laughing.

Notice how the way people walk

      swagger
      mince
      glide
      stride
      inch
            bound   into a room

can tell you everything they want you to know about them.

In like manner tune into yourself.
See how, in so simple a phrase as "Hi,"
you may try to turn on one person
      turn off another
      impress one with your friendliness
      make another feel embarrassed
and so on up and down the interpersonal communicative line.

Notice that in all these instances it is not so much the words or the act

as the intention informing the word and the act

that communicates the message.

Carrythrough in class

Every class period from now on
bring in a phrase of intention that you either said or overheard.

> You overhear in a restaurant the following phrase said
> by a woman to her male companion:
> "Sure, I think you should go out with other women."

Perform this phrase for the class realizing the woman's intention.

The time spent performing these intentions at the start of each
class period will be minimal. If each class member brings in one
intention to perform, the total time given over to intentions will
probably not exceed five minutes. This will not interfere with the
ongoing acting designs but will instead highlight them by
continually reminding you of the significance of intentions.

Carrythrough with script

At each moment of the play's life you must know your character's intention.

Sometimes this happens intuitively.
So firm is your sense of your character
            the other character
            the situation

that you play the right intention without a second thought.

47

Other times the situation will be foreign to you.
In order to figure out your intention
you will have to puzzle over, analyze, and dissect the moment.

However you arrive at your choice of intention, *know*
that there is no one intention that is right for one action
                   for one play
                     for all time.

Things are more relative in the theatre: one actor with one
director in a play might decide a particular intention is right for
a line, and another actor with another director might decide
that a very different intention is right for that same line in that
same play.

Let's look for a moment at Shaw's *Caesar and Cleopatra*.

At the start of the play
Caesar enters and addresses the sphinx.
The young Cleopatra has been sleeping on the sphinx and
awakens to discover this strange person.
Not having the faintest idea who he is she calls out:
"Old gentleman."

Her intention might be

    to let him know that she is listening
    so he won't babble on
    or
    to let him know she is there and a most interesting creature
    so he should come join her.

Caesar answers: "Immortal Gods!"

His intention might be

    to appeal to the sphinx gods to help him
    or
    to admit to the sphinx gods that he is weaker than they
    so they won't harm him.

Cleopatra continues: "Old gentleman, don't run away."

Her intention might be

    to convince him she won't harm him
    so he will come back and keep her company
    or
    to show him she is Queen
    so he must do what she says

or
to let him know he is in a dangerous place
(because there are Romans around who might eat him)
so he'd best not run away.

The point is to decide which intention is right for your character
in that situation
with that director and
h$^{er}_{is}$ concept of the play

and then play that intention truthfully and totally.

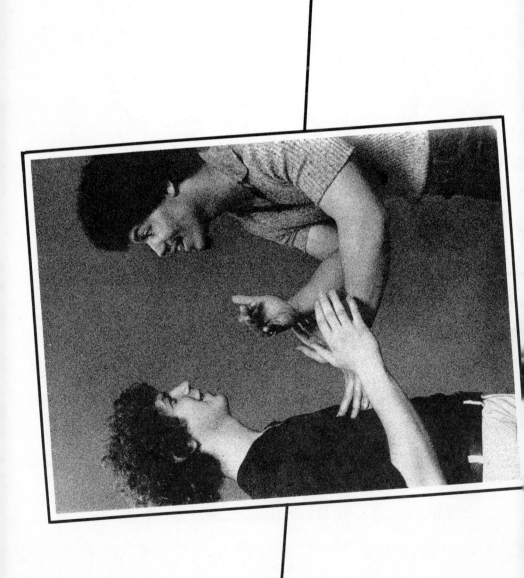

4. Body Acting Centers

Be forewarned.
This chapter is tricky.
More than the others it asks that you accept
and act on
some very unusual propositions.
Bear with it.
What you will have discovered by the end of the designs
will redeem whatever strangeness you felt at their start.

So

go

with

your

adventuresome

spirit

as

you

get

ready

to

experience

your

four body acting centers.

The four centers in your body where
you can initiate and sustain powerful emotion are: stomach

                                        genital

                                        mind

                                        heart.

**You may, of course, have body acting centers other than these four.
If so, use them.
This list is not meant to be exclusive.
Moreover, with but slight modification
the experiences designed to activate these four
could serve equally well to activate others.**

The point now is that
you should learn all you can about body acting centers
so that you can use them when the theatrical occasion calls for it.

You should begin by asking:
What is the distinguishing temper of these acting centers?

You can answer that
by tuning into the center of your body that is most ALIVE

when you are physically
emotionally or
intellectually involved in the world or yourself.

Which body center predominates when
you are immersed in figuring out a problem
step by step
detail by detail?

Quite obviously the

MIND

Mentally alert
all but unaware of the rest of your body,
and unheedful of the events around you,
you are totally absorbed in your work.

Just as you are working at peak capacity,
effortlessly concentrating and beautifully productive,
you might suddenly flash on what could happen to you
if your calculations proved to be wrong.
Suppose you fail?
And other people find out!
The fear of failure now takes hold of you
making you so nervous you can't work.

Your mind is a shambles.
You can't think straight.
You can't think at all!

At this moment your mind center
relinquishes its supremacy to your

STOMACH

which responds to your fear of failure
with "butterfly" sensations.

You now feel uneasy
          jittery
               anxious.

You begin to perspire excessively.
You become giddy
               dizzy
                    weak.

Whatever the exact qualities of the stomach sensation,
one thing is certain:
Butterflies will persist until you rid yourself of anxiety
and restore supremacy to your mind center.

GENITAL

Before discussing the genital center
a cautionary word is in order.

Since childhood most of us have
experienced sexual repression.
Consequently we tend to be self-conscious
about our sexuality.
Notice on late-night talk shows
the giggles and innuendoes,
among even the most sophisticated,
that invariably accompany any mention of sex.

However widespread and understandable
such tittering responses to sex may be,
an actor cannot afford to be embarrassed about
or to deprecate his genital center.

It is a powerful acting center,
electric in its effect on both actor and
audience.

Tune into it.
Learn all you can about it so you can use it on stage
when the dramatic situation calls for it.

The genital center works in this way:

You are talking to someone.

The sound of h^{er}_{is} voice

the way the light sculpts h^{er}_{is} face

the tantalizing way
s/he occasionally reaches out
to touch you

⎱ all
make
you
intensely
desirous
of
h^{er}_{im}.

You want h^{er}_{im}.
Nothing else matters.
Discretion is not important.
Neither is the time of day, the state of the world,
nor jobs waiting to be done.

Such a pleasantly urgent sexual need as this quite obviously signals
that the genital center is dominating you.

Not all genital sensations are so obviously sexual,
although they may have sexual overtones:

You see someone you dislike.
Rage starts in your genitalia and

59

informs your entire being with a steellike strength.
Sparks of electricity fly off an
abrasive, cutting

circle of energy

| Beware trespassers: a person getting angry strength
| from his/er genital center is powerful, not easily subjugated.

HEART

You can best grasp the workings of this center
by using a sense memory:

Think of a time when you felt great pain at someone's leave-taking.
S/he might have left you for another.
S/he might have died.
Whatever the nature of the leave-taking,
you felt pain in your heart.
The pain might have been so great that

you felt your heart would crack
        break
            that it would stop altogether.

Emily Dickinson details with painful precision
such a heart-centered experience in *Parting*:

My life closed twice before its close—
It yet remains to see
If Immortality unveil
A third event to me

So huge, so hopeless to conceive
As these that twice befell.
Parting is all we know of heaven,
And all we need of hell.

You have now been introduced to all the body acting centers.
Before dealing with them in greater detail
three points need to be considered.

1
It is marvelous when you *want* to feel
the particular sensation coming from your body center and
holding you in its sway,
devastating when you do not want so to feel.

61

62

If the aroma of a dinner being set on the table activates
a hunger sensation that will quickly, tastefully be satisfied,
then hunger pains can be pleasant indeed.
But if you are among the two-thirds of the world's population that
goes to bed hungry every night because there is not enough food,
the craving for food is devastating.

But however variable—
even critical—
the effects of your body centers off stage,
on stage you can make them work to your advantage because
you can control them.

2

Thus far
the centers have been dealt with metaphorically:
the term "butterflies" used to describe a stomach sensation
is sentient, not scientific.
"Butterflies" is but a visual and tactile metaphor for the complex way
the stomach might respond to a particular pull of anxiety.
It is on this same metaphoric level that we will continue,
because it is on that level
that the centers are most immediately usable to the actor.

3

In dealing with the centers
allowances will be made for human variability:

since all people are not the same
it is impossible to predict in which body center
a given person will experience a given emotion.

Anxiety was described as originating in the stomach.
But, depending on the person,
that same sensation could just as readily have originated
in another center.

Some people experience anxiety
in their stomach
in their heart
in their genitalia
in their mind

so some people get
ulcers
heart attacks
a spastic colon
headaches

Because of this variability
it is not possible to program exactly how and where
people will feel.

All it is possible to do is to

identify body acting centers

show how particular sensations can be
originated and sustained in these centers

provide designs for activating
these centers and sensations
at will.

It works this way:

You decide on the emotion
your character should be experiencing
in a particular situation.

You determine in which body center
you can initiate and sustain that emotion.

You select an image that
will activate that body center so that
you can actually *experience* the desired emotion
rather than force or pretend it.

It now remains for you to
    learn
      how
        to
          put
            yourself
              in
                such

command of your body acting centers
that
you
can
turn
on
and
turn
off
your own emotions.

Following are experiential designs
directed toward that end.

STOMACH

Preparation: Orchestrating your stomach sensations

List sensations you experience in your stomach:

    butterflies
    nausea
    a comfy warmth

anticipation
the beginning of uncontrollable laughter

| There are more.
| Discover them.

Play your stomach orchestra.

From your own experience or imagination
select an image that will excite your stomach
to experience one of these sensations.

Suppose you want to feel nausea.

In your mind's eye
see a dog just hit by a car.

See the image clearly.
See every detail.
Stay with that image
until you actually feel in your stomach
the revulsion and nausea that image inspires.

Focus on another image that will work for you:

an upcoming painful physical examination
pecan pie with whipped cream
drinking dishwater

See and stay
with each personal image
until you actually experience the sensation
it is selected to provoke.

Remember not to short-cut the route.

Don't go for the feeling.

Always focus on the image.

See the image in exact detail.

Let it inspire the feeling.

Design: Discovering the interior landscape of the stomach

Lie down on the floor.

Close your eyes.

Make yourself TINY
        TINIER
           TINIEST

until you are small enough to enter yourself
through an eye or ear.

Take a body trip
into your stomach.

Refer to pages 23–27
for guidelines to the trip.

Once inside the stomach
explore it.
Get to know it.

Put a stomach-activating image in your mind.

Experience fully
your stomach's response to that image.

Put another image in your mind.

Experience
your response to that image.

Go on to another image.

The difficult part of this design is being in the classroom and
imagining you are inside your body experiencing its reactions to
sensations.

But difficult as it is
you must be prepared to make those imaginary leaps. It is
essential training for stage work, where again and again you
will be called upon to imagine one thing is another
                                one place is another
and then truthfully respond to that transformation.

A bang on a pipe
becomes
a thunderstorm
that terrifies you.

A friend
walking up the stairs
becomes
the ghost of your father.

In these and countless other instances
you must look at one thing,
transform it into something else, and then
truthfully respond to the transformation.

There is always this polarity, this duality. You always know that
the thing to which you are responding is not real, yet so artfully
do you invest the imaginary thing with evocative qualities that
you respond believably to it.

Design: Producing intention at one with stomach sensation

Find a partner.

Put a stomach-activating image in your mind

   walking barefoot in slime.

Talk to your partner about how sick you feel.

Intention: to get him to feel sympathy for you
   so s/he will help you.

Design: Producing intention at odds with stomach sensation

In the preceding design there is a direct line between
your feelings and your intention.
But there are times on stage (as off) when
your feeling is at odds with your intention.

You may smilingly say to someone,
"Yes, do come over.
I would love to see you again soon."

   But you do not want to see that person.
   Ever again.

Your stomach is doing flip-flops
at the very thought of another confrontation.

You may say very casually,
"Why, no.
I don't believe I have met Mr. Adams.
How do you do?"

But this man to whom you so easily extend your greetings
is in reality the person you have schemed to meet.
Actually, meeting him puts you in a state of intense anticipation
which you try to hide by acting as casual as possible.

You may say innocently to someone,
"Oh, I hadn't thought of that."

But you had thought of precisely that.
You are working very hard at sounding like the ingénue,
when in reality you are many points ahead in the game,
shrewdly calculating.

As an actor in these polar situations,
you do not have to *pretend to feel* any of these sensations that
are the emotional underpinnings of your action (your subtext).

72

Your imagination can so excite you that you actually *feel* one thing
while you act to convince the character opposite you
that you feel another, very different thing.

On stage this duality—
this feeling-at-odds-with-intention—
is as exciting
as it is true to the life of our own complex emotionality.

Here's how to do it:

Select and maintain in your mind an image

    an upcoming examination

that will excite your stomach to experience a particular sensation

    anticipation.

Find a partner.

    Carry on a conversation with him
    in which you try to act as casual as possible.

    Talk about the weather or clothes.
    Never let him know the test is worrying you.

State of feeling: anticipation.

Intention: to convince the other you are calm
    so s/he won't condescend to you.

Continue the conversation
in which you feel one thing
but intend another
for at least ten minutes.

This duality of feeling one thing
and intending another
is very common on stage.

Hedda Gabler
is intensely jealous of Thea
yet her intention is to convince Thea
that she likes her immensely.

Hamlet
loves Ophelia
yet he must convince her
that he does not care for her.

Joan of Arc
experiences all the feelings of a woman
yet she must convince the soldiers
she is a man.

73

———— This duality
of feeling and intention
creates extraordinary excitement on stage.

———— So master the technique.
It will stand you in good stead later.

The designs for the three remaining acting centers
follow the same dynamics as those used to activate
the stomach center.

GENITAL

Preparation: Orchestrating your genital sensations

List sensations you experience in your genitalia:

frustration
intense sexual need
pleasant sensuality
rage
flirtation

Play your genital orchestra.

Select a specific image that will excite your genitalia
to experience one of these sensations.

In your mind's eye
see a person you despise.

See the person in the act of doing the hated thing.
See that image very clearly.
Let it evoke the desired hatred
that had its beginning stirrings
in your genitalia.

Erase the image.

Focus on another personal image and stay with it until
it arouses in your genitalia
the desired response.

Design: Discovering the interior landscape of the genitalia

Take a body trip
inside your genitalia.

While you are there
put a genital-activating image in your mind.

Experience
your genital response.

75

Put another image in your mind.

Experience
your response to that image.

Go on to yet another image.

Design: Producing intention at one with genital sensation

Find a partner.

Put a genital-exciting image in your mind

walking barefoot in sand
with someone you desire.

Talk to your partner about how attractive s/he is.

Intention: to get h$_{im}^{er}$ to feel as sensual as you
so you can get physically close to h$_{im}^{er}$.

Design: Producing intention at odds with genital sensation

Select and maintain in your mind an image

someone whispering in your ear

that will excite your genitalia to experience a particular sensation

desire.

Find a partner.

Imagine s/he is the person you desire.

Carry on a conversation with him.
Play hard to get.
Try to convince him that you are immune to his charms.

State of feeling: desire for the other.

Intention: to convince the other that you are uninterested
so s/he will become the more interested.

___ Play off any exciting stimulus
in your immediate environment
___ to increase your feeling of desire.

Continue the conversation
in which you feel one thing
but intend another
for at least ten minutes.

78

HEART

Preparation: Orchestrating your heart sensations

List sensations you experience in your heart:

    love
    longing
    admiration
    sadness

Play your heart orchestra.
Select a specific personal image that will excite your heart
to experience one of these sensations.

    In your mind's eye
    see the image of a person whom you greatly admire;
    when you think about this person
    you are inspired to be better than you are.

    See h^{er}_{im} very clearly.
    Let h^{er}_{is} image evoke the desired response
    in your heart.

Stay with that image for a while.

Erase it.

Go on to yet another image.

Design: Discovering the interior landscape of the heart

Take a body trip
inside your heart.

While you are there
put a heart-activating image in your mind.

Experience
your heart's response.

Put another image in your mind.

Experience
your response to that image.

Go on to yet another image.

Design: Producing intention at one with heart sensation

Find a partner.

Put a heart-exciting image in your mind

a person you admire.

Talk to your partner about h$_{im}^{er}$.

State of feeling: admiration.

Intention: to get your partner to admire the person as much as you do.

Design: Producing intention at odds with heart sensation

Select and maintain in your mind an image

someone you love

that will excite your heart to experience a particular sensation

jealousy.

Find a partner.

Imagine you are jealous of h$_{im.}^{er.}$

Carry on a conversation in which you try to conceal your jealousy.

State of feeling: jealousy.

Intention: to conceal the jealousy.

Continue the conversation
in which you feel one thing
but intend another
for at least ten minutes.

MIND

Preparation: Orchestrating your mind sensations

List sensations you experience in your mind:

concentration
confusion
lightheadedness
headaches
alertness
the energy that comes from problem solving
the excitement of mind involvement
drunkenness

Play your mind orchestra.

Select a specific personal image that will excite your mind
to experience one of these sensations.

Think about a problem
that has been vexing you for a while.

Focus on it.
Recall and relive each aspect of the problem.

Stay with the problem until
it evokes the desired total mental involvement from you.

Erase the image.

Go on to yet another image.

Design: Discovering the interior landscape of the mind

Take a body trip
inside your mind.

While you are there
put a mind-activating image in your mind.

Experience
your mind's response.

Put another image in your mind.

Experience
your response to that image.

Go on to yet another image.

Design: Producing intention at one with mental sensation

Find a partner.

Select a mind-stimulating image

exciting dialogue with a person you respect.

Let your partner become that person and
carry on such a dialogue with h^{er}_{im}.

Intention: to get h^{er}_{im} to feel the same keen mental stimulation you feel
so that s/he will perform well and
excite you the more.

Design: Producing intention at odds with mental sensation

Select and maintain in your mind an image

a martini on an empty stomach

that will excite your mind to experience a particular sensation

drunken lightheadedness.

Find a partner.

Carry on a conversation with h$^{er}_{im}$ in which
you try to convince h$^{er}_{im}$ you are sober.

Continue the conversation
in which you feel one thing
but intend another
for at least ten minutes.

CARRYTHROUGH

Tune into yourself.

List the images that can activate each of your body acting centers.
Now note those times when your stomach commands
your mind is in control
you are bestirred by genital impulses
your heart rules.

Once a particular center has dominance
put an image in your mind
that will activate a different center:

If your stomach is telling you
it's time to eat

make a detailed list of things
you have to do next week.

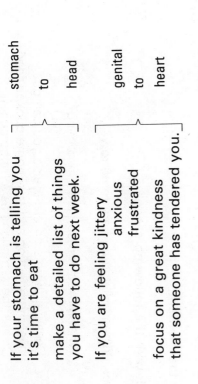

stomach

to

head

If you are feeling jittery
anxious
frustrated

focus on a great kindness
that someone has tendered you.

genital

to

heart

Know that just as you can learn to control and orchestrate your centers in workaday situations off stage, so can you orchestrate them in dramatic situations on stage.

CARRYTHROUGH WITH SCRIPT

Analyze the play.

Determine times a body acting center of your character is producing a particular emotion.

Determine in which of your body acting centers you can initiate and sustain that same emotion.

Activate the appropriate center to produce the emotion.

The situation and images of the play
may provide all the stimulation that you need

_____ or

you may have to substitute a personal image or situation
in order to activate your center to produce the desired emotion.

Determine whether your character's intention is to reveal or conceal
that s/he is in the grips of the emotion produced by the center.

Play the moment.

Try it with the following scene.

ADRIAN   When will you be here tomorrow?

JIM   What makes you so sure I'm coming?

ADRIAN   Because there's no place else you can get
love and affection and free home-cooked food.
Or has the symphony as a fringe benefit.

JIM Hardly.
I should just lock myself in a closet
and practice till my lips fall off,
but I'll probably be here around eight.
That's not a promise, o.k.?
If I don't practice I'm going to be out of a job
and that's no good for either of us.

ADRIAN So come early and practice here.

JIM I can't because I have to pack.

ADRIAN Pack? o.k., what's up?

JIM It's a surprise.

ADRIAN Tell me. *(She tickles him.)*

JIM *(Laughing.)* o.k., o.k.!
I found someone to sublet my apartment.
I'm yours.

ADRIAN Oh, Jim.

JIM   Come on. You're supposed to be ecstatic.
No more seeing each other only when our schedules permit.
No more waiting around.

ADRIAN   Did you already sublet the apartment?

JIM   This guy is definitely interested.

ADRIAN   We've been through this before.

JIM   And I'm taking action now.

ADRIAN   Don't you think we should talk about it?

JIM   No, I don't.
We've talked about it and talked about it,
and I'm still living on the other side of the city.
It's more expensive.
It consumes time neither of us has to spare.
It is not that much different from . . . .
well, I don't want to go through this again.
You know all my arguments.

ADRIAN   I'm just not ready.

JIM   You don't want me to move in.

ADRIAN It's not that.

JIM You do want me to move in.

ADRIAN I don't know.

JIM Look, Adrian, this is ridiculous.

ADRIAN I know it's ridiculous.

JIM Then for god's sake make a decision.
That's all I want.

ADRIAN I'm too tired.

JIM Adrian.

ADRIAN Can you just wait one more day?

JIM No.

ADRIAN Well, I can't make the decision right now.

JIM Every time it ends this way.

ADRIAN Tomorrow.
I promise. Really. Really.
Eight o'clock?

JIM I can't force you to make a decision.
I'm warning you though, it's getting to the point
where I don't care.

ADRIAN *(Pausing.)* Eight o'clock?

JIM I guess.

ADRIAN I love you.

JIM Tomorrow.

Your analysis of this scene could lead you to decide that

Adrian: a. At the start of the scene
she has a genital center.

b. As she playfully tries to seduce Jim
into coming over the next night,
her intention is to reveal her center.

c. When she finds out that Jim is planning on moving in, she gets a sinking sensation in her stomach,

d. which she tries to conceal because she doesn't want Jim to know how much this upsets her.

Jim: a. At the start of the scene Jim has a head center. He is thinking about practicing and packing. He wants to surprise her with his planned move in and is planning how he will do it.

b. He playfully intends to let Adrian know he is thinking about things other than being with her the next night.

c. When Jim senses Adrian's indifference, he might get a stomach or genital annoyance.

d. He chooses to let her know he is annoyed.

In playing the scene, use either the moment-to-moment emotional reality of the given circumstances of the scene to activate your body acting center to produce the desired emotion and/or

use tools you learned in this chapter and substitute one of your personal images to activate a center to initiate and sustain an emotion

and/or

use any combination of playing off the given circum-stances and substituting your own images to produce desired states of feeling.

Make your decision.

Play the scene,
feeling rather than faking
the emotions called for.

Live a full life on the stage.

5. encounter the play

Off stage we act a good deal of the time.

We act the role of subordinate to a person—
often a boss or teacher—
who we in no way feel is superior to us.

We act disinterested in someone
we fear interests us far too much for our own good.

We act happy when we are sad
alert when we are tired

full when we are hungry
understanding when we are annoyed
innocent when we are guilty
out of love when we are in love
in love when we are not.

In all these off-stage dramas there seem to be three principal motives prompting us to act:

We act to affect another.
We act to convince that person of something that is not quite true.
We act to persuade h$_{im}^{er}$ to act.

A teacher whose class you did not attend yesterday (because you did not have your work prepared) passes you in the hall.
You are afraid s/he will be angry with you, so you look apologetic and concerned as you say, "I'm sorry I wasn't in class yesterday. Something happened."

Your motivations:

To affect h$_{im}^{er}$.

Your actions:

You assume the apologetic tone and concerned manner to make h$_{im}^{er}$ feel sorry for you.

To convince him/her of something that is not quite true.

Your statement, manner, and tone imply that what happened to you was quite grave and beyond your power.

To persuade him/her to act.

You hope that as a result of your tone and words the teacher will forget his/her anger at your absence and act favorably toward you in the future.

Untrained actors though we may be,
we are frequently very successful in these off-stage dramas,
as are other people when they act for us.
Is it too extravagant to suppose that much of the fabric of interpersonal communication is woven from such histrionic threads:
"You act for me
and I'll act for thee,
and in our acts we'll flattered be?"

Whatever the frequency and success of our off-stage dramas, once we get on stage we are not always so successful. Ironically, we have difficulty doing on stage what we do off stage so persistently and so well.

Why the difficulty?

The main reason is that on stage we tend to ignore the principal motivation of our off-stage behavior: *We do not act for the other person.*

Thus begins the ironic chain of events:

If we do not act for the other person
we have no one to act for save ourselves.
Once we become absorbed in acting for ourselves
we become so self-conscious that we can't act at all.

How do I look?
How do I sound?
Am I believable?
What gesture should I use here?
Will I forget my lines?
Will so-and-so like me?

Concerns such as these race through our minds making us stilted, mannered, and quite unbelievable.

How do we rid ourselves of this crippling self-consciousness?

One sure way is to remember to act on stage as we do off stage:

Act for the other person.

Yet how often the rehearsal process itself encourages us to do the exact opposite! Instead of prompting us to act for the other person, it prompts us to act for ourselves.

It usually happens like this: At the first rehearsal the director and cast assemble for a readthrough of the play. The director looks authoritatively on while the cast members sit around a table, scripts in hand, and read the roles in which they have been cast.

The supposition here is that from this initial readthrough the actors will begin to get an awareness of the life of the play. But such is not the case!
More often than not

each player is so nervous and/or so wants to impress the director and other actors with h^er_is ability to act that s/he doesn't listen to the play as it is being read. S/he does not stay *here and now* and allow each moment of the play's life to *happen* to h^im. Instead s/he is well ahead in time—planning how to deliver h^er_is next speech.

In this excessive concern with self,
the actor closes h^im_self almost entirely not only to the play
but to what acting is all about:

99

*influencing and being influenced by the other characters
via the medium of the play.*

If your acting work on the play begins like this
how is it going to end?

What you must remember when you do a play is that
the time for self-awareness is in the training process
both before and after your work on the play.
It is then that you are obliged to tune into your own voice
                                        body
                                            imagination

to make them ready for the event of the play.

*But for that discrete period of time
when you are dealing with the play
you must put concern for self aside.*

*Rehearsal is the time to tune out of yourself and
                                    into the play.*

Stated in greater detail, rehearsal is the time to turn your
attention exclusively toward your character, the other
characters, and the theatrical process by which you make
life-charged relationships believable—and exciting—to other
actors and to the audience.

Preparation: HERE and NOW

Find a partner.

Sit on the floor
    cross-legged
    at arms' length from your partner
    facing h^{er}_{im}.

Your body should not suggest a character attitude or
                slump
                lean
                    collapse.

Instead
assume a neutral position with legs crossed
                        shoulders squared
                        back erect
                            hands resting easily on legs.

This position may be uncomfortable if you are used to sitting in a
chair with your legs crossed or your body slouched. If you find
this neutral position too uncomfortable, both you and your
partner should take yourselves through a relaxation exercise:

Imagine you are in a warm rain shower
(the kind you used to play in when you were a kid).

It is washing away all physical
and mental tension.

Let the rainwater run over you,
washing away the tension in your scalp and neck.

Let the water trickle down your body,
washing away tension in your shoulders, chest, and arms.

Throughout this process of washing away tension you and your
partner continue looking at one another. Do not resist being
there, opposite one another.

Continue to allow the water to trickle down your body
washing away tension in your thighs, legs, and feet.

Once the rain is over
splash about in the puddles.

You are ready to continue your preparatory exercise
for encountering the play.

Continue to regard your partner and think about nothing other than
what is happening now—at this moment
                                    in this space
                                            with this person.

As you look at the other,
do not try to communicate nonverbally or
to judge h$^{er}_{im}$ in any way.
Simply be there.
Regarding h$^{er}_{im}$.
Sharing h$^{er}_{is}$ space as s/he shares yours.

You are here.
Right now.
In the dead center of reality.
In the immediacy of experience.
You are open to each new moment as a new moment in time.

This is a new moment . . . .

This is a new moment . .

This is a new moment.

There is only now.
There is a person opposite you.

103

Facing you.
Regarding you.
Being HERE and NOW with you.
Experiencing each moment with you.
You share this space with h$_{im}^{er}$.
No questions asked.
No conditions imposed.

The moments continue to pass.
You continue to experience each passing moment
and the other's presence.

You may find as you sit there that you or your partner gets an irresistible urge to laugh or to cry. If your partner should laugh, grant h$_{im}^{er}$ that right and continue to regard h$_{im}^{er}$, waiting for h$_{im}^{er}$ to recover. Do not break. Do not bring past events into your mind in order to judge h$_{im}^{er}$. Do not think, when s/he laughs, "S/he is ridiculing me." You might feel this because laughter in past experiences has meant ridicule, embarrassment, silliness, etc. Rather than getting caught in the illogical round of judging the present by the past, simply allow h$_{im}^{er}$ to laugh and accept that laugh as what it is at this moment: a person trying to come to terms with sitting still opposite another person, sharing this space with h$_{im}^{er}$, and staying HERE and NOW.

Likewise if you laugh or cry the other person should not leave HERE and NOW to judge you. S/he should grant you the right to your expression. S/he must know that you are laughing neither at h[er][im] nor because of h[er][im]. You are simply trying to come to terms with the exercise. S/he should continue to regard you as you will continue to regard h[er][im].

Both of you stay HERE and NOW.

Both of you continue to experience to the full the reality of each passing moment.

And that is all.

After you have done this exercise for about ten minutes you are ready to

ENCOUNTER THE PLAY.

The following designs are ways to protect you from your own self-consciousness. They are ways of assuming and assuring openness before the written text. They are ways of facilitating natural, instantaneous responses from you to the other actor, from h[er][im] to you, and from both of you to the play.

Design: Solitary encounter

Select a play (if you are a beginning actor it should be one close to your experiences in terms of language and age of characters.)

Read the play
    carefully
      slowly.

Stay HERE and NOW as you read it.

Allow each moment of the play to work its power on you.

Design: Shared encounter

You and a fellow actor
choose a scene from the play you read in the previous design.

Choose a character.

If the teacher-guide selects the play to be enacted and then does not assign roles and scenes until after you have read the play, so much the better. That will help you concentrate on the play instead of concentrating on how you will be in the play.

Resist any and all preconceptions about how you are
going to act the part. Leave yourself open to discovery.
Learn to trust your own understanding and inspiration as
well as those of your fellow actor.

You have read the play
        selected a scene
        selected a character.

But you have not done any more work on the play or
                                    your character.

Now, wide open to experience

Hold the script in your hand.

Sit in a chair
directly opposite the person with whom you are doing the scene.

Regard h^{er}_{im}.
Establish eye contact with h^{er}_{im}.
Look at h^{er}_{im}.
Let h^{er}_{im} look at you.
Look at one another in this easy, accepting way
        until you feel no strain being with one another.

Stay HERE and NOW.
Continue to do so throughout the encounter.
The sole purpose of this experience is for you to
give life to and *take life from your partner—*
and for h$^{er}_{im}$ to do the same with you.

The life that each of you gives and takes
will be the life of the scene.

To this communicative end
study your first speech
until you get the sense of it and
until you can say it to the other person
without referring to the script.

| Whenever you speak to the other person
| you must look at h$^{er}_{im}$.

Speak the speech as *you* would speak it,
not as you think your character would speak it.
Now is not the time to make character choices.
That will come later.
Now you are concerned only with communicating simply and truthfully
the idea in the script to your partner.
You are only a responsive medium
through which the message of the play is relayed.
So don't act the speech.

SAY IT.

As you communicate to your partner
you may find yourself forgetting
        and paraphrasing some of the exact words.

That's all right.
You might even forget everything
and have to look at the speech.
That's all right too.
Should you find it necessary to refer to the script
in the middle of a speech, simply stop speaking.
Look at the printed page.

Try not to break the rhythm of communication; for example,
don't snap your fingers and say by the gesture, "Darn it. I
forgot." If you forget, simply lower your eyes to the printed page
and refresh your memory.

Feel free at any time to stop speaking to your partner
and refer once again to the printed page.
S/he will continue to look at you as you study the script
so the bond of communication will not be broken.

Study the speech as long as you need to
But do not say anything while your eyes—

and attention—
are directed toward the page.

Once you are ready to speak again,
take your attention away from the script and
direct it exclusively toward your partner.
Wait to communicate aloud until, once again,
you can look your partner full in the eyes.

Wait until you are ready to be with h$^{er}_{im}$

    look at h$^{er}_{im}$

        give life to h$^{er}_{im}$

           take life from h$^{er}_{im}$.

While you are speaking to the other person, looking at h$^{er}_{im}$, s/he,
in turn, must be looking at you. At no time while you are
speaking can s/he look down at h$^{er}_{is}$ next speech, preparing
h$^{er}_{im}$self to deliver it. S/he must be as open to you as you were to
h$^{er}_{im}$.

S/he must hear the play's words and sense
truly hear them
so they can work their power on h$^{er}_{im}$

inspiring him/her to feel
inspiring his/her responses to flow naturally from him/her to you.

When you have finished your first speech, continue
looking at your partner while s/he looks down—for the
first time—to study his/her speech. Like you, s/he should take
all the time s/he needs with the speech. Then s/he should
say it to you, as s/he himself/herself would say it.

Not act it.
Say it.

Let your response to his/her words and sense come naturally.
Don't act your response.
Let it flow.
Trust that it will.
All you have to do is listen to this person
whose sole reason for being at the moment is
to give life to and
take like from you
via the medium of the play.

This is the process the two of you are to use as you work your
way through all the pieces of dialogue in your chosen scene.
Don't be concerned about how long it takes. It may take you two
hours to get through a tiny scene. There might be many

111

interruptions as one of you says to the other: "Wait. I didn't feel you were talking to me that time. Let's have another go at it." But when the exercise is over, you will have begun to grasp what that scene—and acting—are all about. You will have begun to:

break down the barrier of self-consciousness as you direct your interest away from yourself and toward the play and your fellow actor

develop a bond of trust and communication with your fellow actor

know the content of the scene

give life to and take life from your fellow actor via the medium of the script

experience each moment of the play's life.

Once you have completed your first shared encounter with the scene try the following variations of it, all of which, like the first encounter, are designed to inspire a natural, meaningful, dynamic relationship between you and the other actor and

between the two of you and the play—a relationship as
unencumbered as possible by excessive self-consciousness.

Variation: Whispered encounter

Follow the directions for the first *shared encounter* with the text
with one exception:

This go round
whisper your speeches.

Make certain in this whispered encounter that
you are not merely speaking low instead of whispering.
To get the full benefit of this encounter, you must whisper.

———— While you are whispering, be sure you don't tense up your
throat. Tensing your throat constricts the voice muscles and
harms your throat. Your throat must be opened. Relaxed. Free of
tension. There is no need to put stress on the throat; your
whispered voice, like your regular voice, comes from the
diaphragm. The throat is simply a highway through which your
voice travels.
————

When the whispered encounter is over, discuss with one
another and the class what each of you discovered.

Whatever else may have happened between the two of you, you should have experienced the following (if you did not, repeat this encounter before going on to the next):

Due to the low vocal volume of this encounter, you and your partner should have been forced to pay even closer attention than before to what each other said.

Your attention should not have wavered. Not even for a moment.

That attitude of excited, attentive listening—as if everything were happening for the first time—is the attitude you must have in stage life.

The whispering should have promoted an even greater bond of intimacy between you and your partner.

Due perhaps to past associations with whispering, the whispered words should have carried with them an air of great significance, rendering the play—and the players —greatly significant. This is as it should be, for if the play and the players are not greatly significant why should anyone bother to attend the performance?

Stage life is committed life.
Whispering is but one way to evoke commitment.

Variation: Back-to-back encounter

Follow the directions for the first shared encounter with the text with two exceptions:

Rather than sit in a chair
lie on the floor
    back to back
    bodies touching.

Unable to look at one another,
you must now establish your communicative bond
exclusively with your voice and bodies.

Even though the back-to-back encounter makes it impossible for you to have eye contact, you are not to look at the script while you are communicating it or while it is being communicated to you. As in the other encounters:

Study the speech.

Look up.

Then say it as you, yourself, would say it.

The other should listen to what you have to say.

Then study his$_{\text{is}}^{\text{er}}$ speech.

Look up.

Say it.

Once you have the design for this encounter firmly in mind, do the encounter.

When you finish, once again discuss the interpersonal and textual discoveries the two of you made during this encounter.

Two important objectives should have been realized. If they were not, or were not realized fully, repeat the encounter.

Because you were lying back to back—
open and vulnerable,
touching each other—
you should have attained an even greater degree of trust and intimacy than you had heretofore attained.

In fact,
the power of your bodies touching,
coupled with your mutual desire to
give life to and
take life from each other
via the medium of the play
should have established as strong a communicative bond as
seeing one another did in the first two shared encounters.

If the desire to communicate is there, touch and sound can
forge bonds equal in their communicative strength to sight.

If, however, the desire to communicate is not there (if you
are too concerned with yourself to devote your energies to
communicating with one another) neither touch nor sound
nor sight nor anything else will forge a communicative
bond.

In the back-to-back encounter the words each of you said
and the way you said them should have assumed an
additional level of importance. Unable to see the other's
facial expression when s/he was communicating and
unable to use your own facial expression when you were
communicating should have made you direct all your
communicative energy to your voice.

Forced in this way to rely on your voice, you should have found and used vocal resources you didn't know you had. You should have stretched your vocal capabilities and effectiveness.

However, because your sole desire was to communicate the life of the play you should have been rescued from becoming that phony actor who is more interested in the sound of his own voice than in its communicative power.

Variation: Distant encounter

Again follow the directions for the first shared encounter, but this time:

Stand rather than sit and
position yourselves at opposite ends of the room.

A room apart

script in hand

do the encounter.

The demands on your voice are slightly more than in the former shared encounters with the play. Take yourself through a vocal warm-up (see page 5) to make certain that your instrument is ready to perform. If at any time during this encounter you discover that your throat is tensing up

STOP THE ENCOUNTER.

Holding your shoulders still,
make complete circles with your head:

Drop your head forward so that your chin rests on your chest

Circle your head to the right so that your ear is almost parallel with your right shoulder

Continue to rotate your head back so that the back of your head is almost parallel with the floor (keep your mouth open so that no tension is put on your neck)

Continue rotating your head until your left ear is almost parallel with your left shoulder

Complete the rotation by circling your head to the right until your chin rests on your chest.

Repeat this exercise two or three times then rotate your head to the left.

Continue to rotate your head first to the right
then to the left

and let an easy, warm stream of sound
initiate in your diaphragm
and pass through your throat.

Breathe when you want as you continue the exercise until your throat and neck are totally relaxed.

After you have completely relaxed your throat
return to the encounter and
complete the scene.

Putting distance between the two of you should have made you strengthen even more the communicative powers of your voice. Also, because your desire was to communicate with your partner—because, therefore, you were not self-consciously focusing on yourself—you undoubtedly behaved with natural appropriateness to the situation.

Once again, if you did not make the discoveries cited above, you should repeat this shared encounter. Then you should repeat any (or all) of the shared encounters with the play until you feel secure about them.

Check yourself by asking the following questions:

Have I broken down the barrier of my self-consciousness by directing my interest away from self (insofar as possible) and toward my fellow actor and the action of the play?

Have I developed a bond of trust
                  intimacy
                        communication

with my fellow actor?

Have I given life to and taken life from my fellow actor via the medium of the script?

Have I expanded the communicative powers of my body and voice?

Do I know the action of the scene?

Have I experienced each moment of the scene's life?

_____

You may have earned an additional benefit by completing successfully these shared encounters with the play. You may now know the scene without ever having committed it to memory in the old drone way. To be sure, some speeches may still require more work before they are yours letter-perfect, but your grasp of the material should now be almost as sound as it is natural.

Carrythrough

Do the HERE and NOW exercise as often as you can with anyone who will do it with you. A friend (better yet an enemy) is a perfectly suitable partner. Whether or not that person is in theatre is entirely irrelevant.

Once you find a partner do the following:

Sit in a neutral position
    in a chair or   ⎤
               ⎬ facing one another.
    on the floor   ⎦

Regard one another for ten minutes.
(Try not to flinch, scratch, blink unnecessarily.)

Stay HERE and NOW.
Think about nothing other than what is happening now.
At this moment.
With this person.

Do not communicate nonverbally with one another.
Simply *be* there,
sharing one another's space,
experiencing to the full each moment as it happens.

Don't allow anything the other person does
to take you out of HERE and NOW.

Every time you do the HERE and NOW exercise
try to increase the length of time you regard one another.
Staying HERE and NOW,
experiencing to the full each discrete moment as it happens,
strive for twelve minutes
then fifteen
then eighteen.
Persevere until you can stay HERE and NOW for an hour
opposite another person.

Now for the acid test.
Suppose you're in rehearsal for a play.
The director yells at you

embarrassing you
making you want to cry
or run away
or hit h$_{im}^{er}$.
Do none of these.
Don't yell back or allow yourself to pout.
Simply stay HERE and NOW as s/he yells at you.
Allow h$_{im}^{er}$ this expression of hostility.
But don't allow h$_{im}^{er}$ to upset you.
Nothing will be gained by becoming resentful.
Don't allow the chastisement to stay with you.
Stay HERE and NOW.
As soon as the director has finished h$_{is}^{er}$ tirade forget what happened.
Continue your work.

Of course after the rehearsal—
after you have successfully completed your work—
you can go up to the director and discuss whatever problem
prompted h$_{is}^{er}$ explosion. In this way both of you can solve the problem
rather than become emeshed in a tangle of hurt feelings.

Try this acid test when people off stage attack you in anger.
Stay HERE and NOW until they have finished.
Then deal with the problem.

You can also do a variation of the HERE and NOW exercise by yourself. When a worry from the past pushes its way into your consciousness and prevents you from doing the task at hand, bring yourself (your consciousness) back to HERE and NOW:

One at a time
look at five objects.
Don't just glance at the objects.
Really examine them until you *know*
the physical details of their composition.

Say your name three times.

Pull a hair on your head.

Take and taste a drink of water.

Through this simple exercise you will discover that whatever worry has arbitrarily pushed its way into your consciousness can be pushed out just as arbitrarily. (Of course, at a later time you may wish to bring this worry back to consciousness in order to deal with it and solve it—*when you want to solve it.*)

The point of this exercise is that
you can cultivate the ability to direct your entire consciousness to
HERE and NOW
in order to experience the reality of that moment—
and that moment only—
to the fullest
so as not to be upset over something that just happened
so as not to be anxious about what might happen an hour from now.

6. Search and Research

You have completed your first encounters with the play:

    You have experienced its moment-to-moment reality.
    You have come to terms with it on its most immediate
                            accessible level.

Now that you know the play's topography,
you can investigate the less obvious
but equally meaningful levels of the play's life.

Find out WHEN
       HOW
          BY WHOM the play originated.

Just as you can understand a person better if you know his/her parents and the environment in which s/he developed so can you better understand a play by knowing these same things. To be sure, like the person, the play cannot be summed up or explained absolutely by parentage and formative environment. But insights into its subterranean, inner life can be gained by knowing the forces at work in its formation.

THE PLAYWRIGHT

The playwright created the play's world in which you must live created the play's characters you must become designed the play's actions you must undertake.

Know this creator so you can better understand his/her creation.

Preparation: Researching the playwright

Find out if there is a situation in the playwright's life that the situation of the play echoes. It follows that knowing as much as you can about the former will help you to understand—and act—the latter.

Tennessee Williams's *The Glass Menagerie* and Arthur Miller's *After the Fall* are examples of people and events in playwrights' own lives being the basis for their plays' lives.

Knowing about Williams's youth, the delicacy of his sister Laura, the good-humored but devastating domination of his very southern mother and the inextricable pattern of their lives together help you understand the tragicomic characters in *The Glass Menagerie.*

In the same way knowing about Miller's marriage to Marilyn Monroe and the tortured course of his life during the McCarthy era help you understand better the complex passions in *After the Fall.*

Granted, other plays and characters might not be such intimate expression of the playwright's life. Look then for other kinds of passions that might have charged him to write his play.

Bertolt Brecht's *Joan of the Stockyards* is a searing political manifesto. In this case you want to investigate the playwright's political tenets in order to understand and act their working power in his plays.

August Strindberg wrote his antifeminist *The Father* in response to Henrik Ibsen's profeminist *A Doll's House*. In this case you investigate the provocation in order to better understand the response.

Jean-Paul Sartre used a classical theme to dramatize a present-day crisis in *The Flies*. You first become familiar with the Greek Electra and Orestes. Then you investigate resistance France and Sartre's philosophy to seek out the dark and lonely birth of his existential Electra and Orestes.

Not that when you have finished this kind of research you will be ready to act the play. You could research a play forever and not be able to act it.

Research is not a substitute for doing. It is a preparation.

It is a way to get a handle on the play
    make you feel familiar with it
        help you know it.

This is all-important.
No production ever suffered from the actors' knowing the play too well.

It's when actors have not done their homework that they fall
back on stock tricks, generalizations, and repetitions of past
productions.
It's then that this play begins to look like the play before
        this character like the character before.

Research is a way to get you out of whatever play you did last and
            into the play at hand.

And it is the play at hand that's the thing.

Set no limits on yourself in your getting-acquainted period.
Don't decide, "I'll spend an hour or two and call it a day."
Spend as long as you can and learn as much as you can.

Then let this knowledge become a living part of you.
Let it get hold of you.
The stuff of the play mattered to the playwright
so it must matter to you,
the one who is directly responsible for making it matter to the audience.

133

Unlike some other kinds of research you may have done,
you can make this research live.
This is not research into something out there

                away from you,
                    dead
                        belonging to another time and space.

This is research that you can incorporate into your very self
when you live the life of your character in rehearsals and
                          performances of the play.

Morever, when the performance of the play is over, you will
have not only craft but personal improvement to show for it. As
you know from experience, the more your learning is reinforced
by putting it into practice, the more you remember it. Because
you will have been able to "practice" your research in
rehearsals and performances of the play, you will better
remember what you have learned. Thus your acting research
makes you a richer, more informed person and vice versa.

What a great way to get an education!

How fortunate that you can accomplish two things at once:

What research you do for your craft enriches you.

And whatever research you do for yourself enriches your craft.

Design: Researching the playwright

Take { this set of questions } to the library
{ a notebook }
{ a pen }
and answer the following questions:

When did the playwright live?

Where did s/he live?

What was h$_{is}^{er}$ personal life like?

What were h$_{is}^{er}$ philosophical
political
sexual   passions?

What was the social temper of the time?

What was the political temper of the time?

Did s/he conform to or rebel against society?
If s/he rebelled, what form did the protest take?

What does the playwright say about the play?

What else has aroused your curiosity about the playwright from your work to date?

Satisfy your curiosity by posing and answering more questions.

THE PLAY AND THE CHARACTERS

Just as the playwright needs investigating so do the play and its characters. And the further away in time

space

language the play and its people are from today,

the more necessary the investigation.

It is easier, for example, to relate to Leroi Jones's *Dutchman*, which involves a young black man and a young white girl on a present-day New York subway, than it is to relate to John Webster's *The Duchess of Malfi*, which involves lords and ladies in Renaissance Italy.

However close to your own experience the play may be, some research is probably necessary. For a play is not a novel with long descriptive passages that create in minute, evocative detail the situation, action, and character of the heroes. A play simply plunks you smack-dab in the middle of action, character, and situation, and you are expected to act as that character in such a situation would have acted. Unless you fill in the lines between the lines, this is difficult.

Filling in those lines is what research is all about.

Think of the time you take "researching" your lover.
You try to find out all about h^{er}_{is} family
                       passions
                       preferences
                       past loves.

How much more time you should take to research your character!

Your lover you must simply be *with*.
Your character you must *be*.

Preparation: Researching the play and the characters

How do you go about researching the play and its characters?

One way is to go to *paintings* of the period in which the play is set.
An artist's portrait can tell you a great deal about a person.
And the communication is immediate.

TAKE IN the person in the painting.

    Look at h$_{is}^{er}$ bearing
                 eyes
                 set of the lips.

    Examine h$_{is}^{er}$ clothing.

    Feel h$_{is}^{er}$ attitude.

    Sense h$_{is}^{er}$ sense of self.

BECOME the person in the painting.

    Regard h$_{im}^{er}$ in the same way s/he is regarding you.

    Hold your head as s/he holds h$_{is}^{ers}$.

    Put into your head thoughts you imagine to be in h$_{is}^{er}$ head.

The results of this experiential viewing will be useful to you as an actor.

Personal diaries, autobiographies, and biographies are also intimate, exact sources of character information.

In her notebooks, Anaïs Nin gives some fascinating insights into people in her life, like Antonin Artaud, Henry and June Miller, and other known and not so well-known people of the time.

Simone de Beauvoir tells us much about the French bourgeoisie, to say nothing of Jean-Paul Sartre and Albert Camus, in her three-part autobiography.

Albert Speer gives us a chilling portrait of the German mind in the depression preceding World War II.

Etiquette books, salesmanship manuals, popular romances, catalogues talk not only to but about their era.

These popular documents can provide you with offbeat but actable insights into the people for whom and about whom they were written.

Objects of the time can tell us much.

Helen Hayes once said she discovered an important clue to her character of Victoria Regina while examining the engravings on a virginal (a baroque musical instrument).

Food can inspire.

Alec Guinness drank the tea Hitler drank in his preparation for the role of Hitler.

There seems no end to what can give us insights into character.

Food
music
dance
games
clothing
religion
furniture

all these manifestations of a culture and many more can say important—actable—things to you about the people who lived in the culture.

It seems not too grand to suggest that all art and nature are the actor's province. And this is as it should be. Since it is the actor's charge to put living people on stage for other living people to believe, the actor must know all s/he can about *life*.

Design: Researching the play and the characters

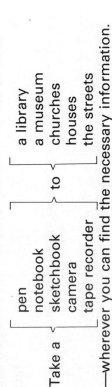

Take a
{ pen
notebook
sketchbook
camera
tape recorder }

to { a library
a museum
churches
houses
the streets }

—wherever you can find the necessary information.

Answer the following questions:

What was the time and place of the play's action?

What were the people like in that year that place?

How did they behave?

How did they dress?

How did they carry themselves because of their dress? (Look at the pictures of the shy, graceful women of the early 1900s who carried their heads cocked under floppy or cloche hats.)

What was their standard of morals?

What was their level of awareness about other people and places?

Were they optimistic or pessimistic about the future of the world and their future in the world?

What was the social caste system of the time?

Once you have a general picture of the people of the time decide how your character fits in or rebels against this world.

If you were playing Alma in Tennessee Williams's *Summer and Smoke*, you would have to know how southern ladies of the time were educated, how they were expected to behave, what their limited possibilities in a "man's" world were, and what the conventional standard of morality was in order to understand and act Alma's complex character.

If you were acting the young, poetic Richard in
Eugene O'Neill's gentle *Ah, Wilderness!* you would
have to know the standard of behavior expected
from young men at the turn of the century in order
to understand how Richard in his youthful, raw
eagerness to discover and savor the world defied
those standards.

Based on what you know about your character
                                want to know about h$^{er}_{im}$

pose more questions.

Answer them.

As you set about answering these questions, as you set about
examining the mind and spirit of the time, you must never, never
learn about your character in order to judge h$^{er}_{im}$.

Don't, for your own sake or for the audience's, point out how
inferior the mind of your character is to your own.
Don't condescend
        compromise
        comment upon your character.
Quite the reverse!

You are doing your research as a preparation for becoming your character.

You are discovering that s/he is
who s/he is
why s/he is.

You are accepting h^{er}_{is} faults
exulting in h_{is}^{er} strengths.

As in a great love affair
so in becoming your character
you are in the process of possessing
and being possessed by your own creation.

CARRYTHROUGH

Make your own private research center.

Get some files with paper pockets.

Label the files according to countries:

United States
France
Russia
England
Latin America
China

Then subdivide each file according to periods:

United States: Revolutionary War
               Civil War
                   1920
                   1930
                   1940
                   1950
                   1960
                   1970

Once the file is ready, get in the habit of clipping out interesting and relevant pictures and articles from magazines and newspapers. Xerox copies of pictures and articles from magazines, newspapers, books you should not cut up. Put your find in the appropriate pocket.

In addition to magazine, newspaper, and book excerpts, you might want to jot down and file your own impressions of people
    events
    exhibits
    movies—
or any experience that gives you vital and potentially usable insights into people you might portray on stage. And you'll be surprised at what might prove useful.

It is reported of Laurence Olivier that whenever he sees a person with an interesting nose he makes a note of it and looks forward to the time he might use that nose for a new character on stage.

The American philosopher George Santayana said that the real reason for possessing good friends lies in what they can help you become. This is the reason for research. Like a good friend it can help you become a richer, better informed actor and a richer, better informed person.

Another American, Martin Luther King, pointed out in an interview the value not only to the theatre but to the world of the well-informed actor. Dr. King was asked what he thought about the fact that actors played such a prominent role in the civil rights movement. The implication of the question was that it would be more dignified were other professions more visible in the movement. Dr. King answered without a moment's hesitation that he could think of no group of people better suited to the cause of civil rights. Were not actors, he asked, people whose very profession it was to understand, empathize with, and act the passions of other people? How natural then that they be the ones to empathize so very immediately and so totally with the problems of the many dispossessed blacks in this country and then *act* upon their understanding.

This is a noble, inspiring idea to carry with you
as you set about the task of making yourself *a more informed actor*
a more informed person.

7. Transformation to character

In the theatre:

The playwright
originates the characters and action that
inspire this multifaceted theatre event.

The director
integrates all these theatrical elements,
creates the *mise en scène,* and
guides the actors in their work.

The set designer
molds a meaningful dynamic environment
in which the action can happen.

The lighting designer
sets moods in light and shadow
and illuminates the action.

The costume designer
sees to it that the play's characters are appropriately clothed
in garments that will move and create interest.

But, finally,
it is the actors
on whom the work of all these other theatre artists depends.
They enter the environment created by their fellow workers and
bring it to life by transforming themselves into characters
in whom the audience can believe and have interest.
Only when that belief and that interest are engendered in the audience
does theatre HAPPEN.

Since transformation
is of such prime importance in the theatre
and since it is the actor's chief responsibility
it bears further detailed and intense investigation:

Specifically, how much do the actors need to change themselves
in order to complete their transformation to character?

Do they change their outside

or their inside

or both?

And how?

Because it is the actors who are responsible for transformation
it is to them we should go for clarification of the term.
At least three actors have talked on the point of transformation
almost as well as they have accomplished it in their extraordinary careers.

Nazimova
said transformation must be *total*:

"I have to reconstruct my whole self
into the woman I am to portray—
speak with her voice,
laugh with her laughter,
move with her motion."

Edith Evans
said transformation must be *real*:

"I try to find the truth and real life in the person . . . .
to make people real people."

And Laurence Olivier
said transformation must be *persuasive*:

"The actor persuades himself first,
and through himself the audience."

If we combine these three statements into one
it would read like this:

Transformation is the total reconstruction of self to character
in order to persuade both self and audience
that the resulting character is A REAL PERSON.

Using this synthesis as your guide,
you can now start the process of transforming yourself to character.

To this end you will undertake a number of designs.

In class—
in your laboratory where you have time to experiment

change

grow

learn—

you should do all the designs, and
you should do them again and again until you have mastered them.

___ In your actual creation of characters for public performance,
    however, you might decide that some designs work well for
    creating certain characters, some work well for creating others.
    Feel free at that time to use only what designs work best for
___ you, and to modify or extend them in whatever way you see fit.

The point now is to master all the designs so that in the future
you will have at your command workable models
for transforming self to character.

Enter each design openly
        naively
            ready to learn.

153

Don't predict or prejudge.

Let each experience speak for itself.

Let each teach you.

Don't just pay lip service to the overused, ill-understood maxim
"learn by doing."
Really LEARN BY DOING.

Preparation: Discover yourself in the character and the character in you

Closely examine your character
as s/he is revealed to you in the play
and your research.

Then list your character's essential states of feeling.

S/he is haughty
buoyant
nervous
ill at ease in company
paranoid
optimistic
vain

Keep this list with you in your notebook so
you can refer to it again as the need arises.

Now discover feelings you yourself have experienced
that are similar to your character's.

Through this process
discover yourself in the character and
the character in you
and form an empathetic bond that makes your character live.

If your examination of the character reveals that s/he is
sad, remember a time when you were as sad or imagine a
time when you could be as sad. Let your emotion validate
and make live in you your character's emotion.

Very important—
don't force your sadness.
Instead,
in as detailed a way as possible
re-create the situation in which you felt sadness
or imagine a situation in which you could so feel.

See that situation.

See each and every detail.

155

Let your memory or your imagination of that situation
pull the sadness from you.

You might remember a time when someone left you,
perhaps for another.
In your re-creation of the leave-taking you would:

See the place where the two of you were
together the last time.
See it as exactly as you can.

If it was inside
see furniture, paintings, dishes;
if outside
the details of the landscape.

Remember odors
sounds
textures.

Remember the time of year.
the time of day.

Remember the degree of light or dark.

Remember what you wore
  what you said
  what you wanted and
  what you got.

See the other person—
see h$_{is}^{er}$ face
  what s/he wore.

Remember the sound of h$_{is}^{er}$ voice
  touch of h$_{is}^{er}$ body.

Remember h$_{is}^{er}$ words
  your answer
  what you wanted to answer.

Once you have re-created this situation in detail
there will be no need to force the emotion of sadness.
The feeling will come now as surely as it came then.

In those explorations of past self or imaginations of probable
self, don't shy away from looking at things about yourself you
would rather forget because they are personally embarrassing
or socially unacceptable.

157

Robin Gammell once said of his extraordinary creation of Hitler in Brecht's The Resistible Rise of Arturo Ui at the Tyrone Guthrie Theatre: "The first thing I did was to discover the Hitler in me."

Don't gloss over your feelings

Don't edit

Don't be kind to yourself

Instead discover
    recognize
    claim   feelings in yourself
        that are similar to your character's,

no matter how odious
      how laughable
      how stupid   these feelings may seem to you.

In the same vein, don't judge the feelings of the character you are creating. Your job is to create these feelings. If there is judging to be done let the audience do it later on, once you have transformed yourself to a true character with real feelings for them to judge.

YOUR CHARACTER AT ANOTHER AGE: COMPLETE THE LIFE CYCLE

Wordsworth once wrote: "The Child is father of the Man." In this simple phrase the poet makes an observation that is most useful to character development for actors: those things children do and have done to them influence the formation of their adult character.

Adopting this observation for stage use, it would be a worthwhile experiment to allow your stage character to develop along the line your own has: from childhood on up. The purpose of this experiment is to make your character more complete for you so you can more completely understand h_{er}im and more completely become h_{er}im.

In this experiment it goes without saying that you can't take the same amount of time to develop your play character as you did your own. For purposes of the stage you must compress select zero in on certain significant events from your character's childhood and avoid others.

Preparation: Become your character as child

For a trial run, look to yourself.
Do you now have any salient characteristics that were formed by
your childhood experiences?

I am neat, almost
compulsively so.

As a child I always had to put my room
in perfect order before I could go out
and play.

I am overly
demonstrative, moved
easily to laughter
    anger
     tears.

When I was growing up, my family was
hyperemotional, given to frequent
outbursts of anger and affection.

→

In this same way look to your
character. Examine h^{er}_{is}
characteristics.

Then figure out in what way these
characteristics might have been formed
by childhood experiences.

Suppose your examination of your character
reveals that s/he is attractive
    shy
    fearful
    excessively dependent on certain people
    resentful
    incapable of sustaining a relationship.

In order to discover what childhood experiences might have helped form these qualities, you can ask the following questions (and any others you consider relevant).

In your questions and answers bear in mind that you are in the process of merging your identity with your character's identity. You are becoming one. So refer to your character in the first person.

As a child, was I shy?   Why?

Did I want to please certain people?   Who? Why?

Was I considered good looking by others?   Why?

Did I think I was good looking?   Why?

What did I fear?   Why?

What did I hate?   Why?

Whom did I love?   Why?

What did I want to be when I grew up?   Why?

What was my relationship with my parents?   Why?

Take time to think about
     assimilate your discoveries about your character as a child:

Lie down.

Close your eyes.

See in your mind's eye a picture of your character
when s/he was a child ten years old or thereabouts.

Project all the ideas and images you have
about your character as a child
into a three-dimensional image—
something like a hologram.

See the image before you.

Open your eyes.
The image is still there.

Step into it.

Become the child of your character
the child of yourself.

Design: Become your character as child—alone and with family

In this design, work either one at a time or
all at the same time—each in your own

circle of solitude

Wake up in the morning in character.

Get dressed.

Think about what you are going to do today.

After you have dressed
go to breakfast in the kitchen or dining room.

163

While you are eating
carry on a conversation with your mother.

You may cast another class member as your mother
or simply imagine her there with you.
If your character's mother would not be there,
imagine whoever could be there with you while
you eat your morning meal—another relative
                                    a friend
                                    a dog
                                    your imagination.

When you talk to that person
the conversation should be a typical one in which
you talk about matters of ongoing concern:

    Cover up why you are not doing well in school.
    Pout your way through a reprimand.
    Tattle on your best friend.

Design: Become your character as child—with other children

All the class members can do this design together.
The more children there are to interact with—
and define yourself against—the better.

Imagine you are in a playground.

Together, as a group,
decide on what things there are in the playground
where they are located.

Here is a pond.

Here are swings.

Here is a place to eat lunch.

Here are _____

_____

_____ and _____

After filling the space of the playground,
decide on an intention
that stems from the needs of your character.

I want to get a particular child to like me.

I want to get even with another child.

I want to con the other kids into playing
a game I think I can win.

I want to keep the children from hurting me as they have in the past.

After you have

stepped into the mental and physical image of your character as a child

transformed the room into a playground

decided on an intention for yourself

begin to pla^y with the other children on the playground.

Let play be a proving ground for character development.

This design will take at least one full class period, maybe longer. Don't rush it. The longer you improvise your character as child the more you will learn about h$^{er}_{im}$.

In all these improvisations
do not "play at" being a child:
don't try to be coy
        cute
        bashful
        awkward.
Only adults see children as "children."

Children see themselves as people
When children are hurt they don't think,
"Oh, well, I'm only a child.
I'll forget this in time."
To a child his hurt, like his joy, is real—
every bit as absorbing as an adult's hurts and joys.

So in these improvisations—or when you are playing a child on stage—enter the mind, spirit, and body of your character with as much integrity and thoughtfulness as you would were you entering the character of Hamlet.

In this improvisation—and all others—don't ever allow yourself to step outside your character to judge it.
Concentrate.
Persevere.
No more than you can suddenly leave your own character can you leave your play character.
You and s/he are one.
If you leave, the character dies.
And rebirth is a long, arduous, risky process.

If despite the best of intentions you feel your concentration wavering, don't panic! Do a variation of the HERE and NOW exercise on pages 101–105.

Other situations
in which to become your character at ten years old:

    a birthday party
    a classroom
    a grocery store
    a soda fountain
    a picnic
    a dentist's waiting room
    church
    the school lunchroom

Design: Become your character at other ages

Discover even more about your character
by entering his/er mind
        body
          spirit when s/he is eighteen
                her/is own age
                a long-living person aged eighty
                another age that reveals character.

In becoming your character at these different ages
follow the same format of *Your Character as Child*:

Review your *Search and Research* into
the life and time of your character.

Ask and answer a series of questions
about your character at each age:

What do I want most in life?   Why?

To what unfulfilled plans
must I resign myself?   How do I resign myself?

About whom or what
do I daydream?   Why?

Decide on an improvisatory situation
in which to become your character.

Situations for your character at eighteen:

informal dance
date
graduation exercises
study hall
beach
slumber or stag party
formal dance

football game
restaurant
alone in your room
rock concert
waiting in line for a movie

Situations for your character at your character's age:

class reunion
party
bull session
dance
theatre lobby
political meeting
picnic
shopping
train ⎤
plane ⎥ ride
boat ⎥
bus ⎦

Situations for your character as a long-living person of seventy or eighty:

in your family home
in a park
at a dinner

in a nursing home
at a meeting
on the street

Fill the space of each situation
with concrete objects appropriate to it.

Decide on an intention for your character in each situation:

I want to remain as inconspicuous as possible
so no one will bother me.

I want to appear vulnerable
so someone will help me.

Lie down on the floor.

Close your eyes.

Formulate a mental and physical picture of yourself.

Project it in space.

Get up.

Step into it.

171

Enter the experience.

Concentrate.

Persevere.

Have fun.

Discover.

Become.

And learn all you can about your character.

Carrythrough: Spend a day as your character

Relying on your growing understanding of your character resulting from the work you have done so far and on your imagination decide how your character behaves in his/her daily life.

Now do some of the things you do every day *but do them in character.*

You might find it useful to do some of these designs with your partner in the scene.

Eat breakfast
lunch or
dinner   in character.

What you eat
Where you eat
How you eat
What you think about while you are eating

will be determined
insofar as possible
by your character.

Get dressed in the morning or
in the evening in character.

In all probability
you will have to wear your own clothes,
so let your imagination transform them.

Dress in the manner and
with the requisite vanity
of your character.

While you are dressing have in mind
your character's attitude toward self:

Is s/he self-deprecating?
vain?
afraid of his/her body?

173

Does s/he enjoy sensuality?
not give a damn about her/his appearance?

Also have in mind your character's intention:

Does s/he want to impress?
make him/herself more sexually appealing?
outrage others with her/his clothes?

Take a walk in character.

Even though you may be on your way to your own destination
imagine you are going somewhere your character would go.

Discover in your walk
the idiosyncratic motion of your character:

Does s/he mince?
make big, aggressive strides?
shuffle?
swing?
bounce?
hide her/himself?
show her/himself off in her/his walk?

Experience your character's *hobbies or pastimes.*

In his spare time does your character read?

                                     paint?
                                       dance?
                                       go to ball games?
                                       hike?
                                       cook?
                                       eat?
                                       write?

Transform yourself to character and
do the hobby or pastime.

If you are playing Stanley Kowalski,
dress like Stanley,
put yourself in Stanley's frame of mind,
and go bowling.

If your transformation is successful, the people at the bowling
alley whom you meet should believe you are, indeed, a Stanley.

Do some *workaday things* you yourself might never do but
your character would do.

Suppose your character is extremely rich and does
nothing to earn a living. Put yourself in the frame of mind

which says that life is your oyster. Spend a day or so lollygagging, doing nothing more strenuous than getting dressed.

If you can spare the time,
spend two hours having a bath
and another three getting dressed.

Spend an hour nibbling tea and toast.

Style your hair
lock by lock
in a new elaborate "do."
As soon as your new coiffure is complete,
it bores you.
Change it.

Take time to extend and answer invitations
love notes
get-well cards.

Or at the other end of the economic extreme, suppose your character is extremely poor and hardworking, responsible for her/his family's survival. Spend a day in which you imagine that you cannot call one second your own. You must work so hard for others in order to survive that

you race from one task to another as though on a treadmill
going full speed.

As you do your work
know that you are in a social class condescended to,
patronized, often despised by the ruling class.

Set time limits for everything you do.
(Use a timer if you have one.)

Shower in three minutes.
Eat in twelve.
Mend clothes (you are going to wear) in six.

If you cook a meal
imagine your every move is being superintended.

Clean the house as if you were cleaning it
for a most meticulous employer.

Whatever your character's social
                              generic
                              economic condition,

step into that reality
and behave accordingly
for a day or as much of a day as you can spend.

177

178

Move with your character's motion.

Talk with your character's speech.

Think your character's thoughts.

Assume your character's attitude.

Should you find while you are experiencing the design that your attention wanders, bring yourself back to the HERE and NOW of your character's reality:

See the world through his/her eyes.

Think his/her thoughts.

Focus on his/her intentions.

There may be times in the previous designs and carrythrough when you purposely put yourself outside the mind and spirit of your character in order to analyze what you are doing.

If you are in the process of discovering the character's walk, you might try one style of walking for a time, decide it's not right,

try another,
then another and another,
until you find the right one.

This process demands
that you step into character to do,
then step out to analyze what you have done,
then once again step back into character
to incorporate what you have learned by doing.

It is important to your progress as an actor that you learn how to
step in and out of character; for not only in your private work on
character but in the public moments of rehearsing and
reshaping the play, you will be required to step into, then out of,
character again and again.

This zigzag process is not so difficult really. You do something
like it off stage all the time.

You are talking to a friend:
    you are easy
        laughing
        playful.
Suddenly a professor happens by

and you become another person: serious
                                respectful
                                controlled.

The professor leaves:
you revert to your talking-to-friend self.

So once again
tune into and use your experience off stage
to help train yourself for the demands of
your on-stage creative process.
In this way train yourself to

quickly step into your character
to do

then just as quickly step out of character
to analyze,
reflect,
listen to criticism

then once again
step back into character
to incorporate what you have learned by doing.

DREAMS

Preparation: Daydream in character

Once again on the basis of your research

        analysis
        understanding
        insight
        imagination

determine what your character's obsessions are: what preoccupies his/her waking and sleeping mind.

Design: Daydream in character

During the day in periods of time when you are not totally engaged in doing your own things, daydream in character.

If you are playing Hamlet you might, at times, excite yourself by daydreaming ways you can successfully avenge the murder of your father.

182

At other times you might torture yourself by daydreaming what is happening sexually between your mother and her new husband.

If you are playing Linda Loman in *Death of a Salesman* you might ease yourself by daydreaming that Willie is doing extraordinarily well at his job and that the family is as happy together now as it was in the past.

Or you might torture yourself by daydreaming what will become of you if Willie never does succeed again.

Learn in this way

how to construct

and feed off

all the levels of consciousness

that occupy and preoccupy
form and inform

the mind of your character.

Preparation: Dream your character's nightmare

What does your character most fear—

    Becoming old?
    Being alone?
    Discovery?
    Failure?

In character imagine that what you most fear comes to pass. This is the nightmare you will experience.

Design: Dream your character's nightmare

This design can be done with the entire class performing at one time, each in his own

circle of solitude

Lie down

Close your eyes

Start to "dream" your character's nightmare

Experience the dream in your mind for a few minutes

Then get up and experience it actually.

Imagine whatever you need for your nightmare experience that does not exist in the room.

Play off the other actors who are experiencing their nightmares simultaneously with yours.

You may decide someone else in the room is a character in your dream (say your mother or your lover). If you talk to him and s/he does not respond, let that rejection deepen your nightmare.

Conversely, if someone comes up to you and calls you by another name, seeing you as a figure in his dream, let that encounter be one of the countless, inexplicable things that happen in dreams.

Use whatever happens to you

as you experience your character's nightmare

in order to come to grips with $\left.\begin{array}{c} \\ \\ \\ \end{array}\right\}$ understand h_{is}^{er} fears.
assimilate

Preparation: Dream your character's best dream

Decide what your character wants most in the world—
what would make h_{im}^{er} supremely happy.

Does s/he want to be famous?

Does s/he want a particular person?

Does s/he want release from an obsession
that is draining h_{is}^{er} life energy?

Design: Dream your character's best dream

Follow the same pattern for this design as you did for the last.

Lie down

185

Start to dream your character's wish fulfillment

Experience the dream in your mind for a few minutes

Then get up and experience it actually.

Transform the room—

Let your imagination supply any needed elements—

Play off the other actors—

EXPERIENCE!

ASSIMILATE!

DISCOVER!

KNOW!

ANIMAL OR INSECT

Preparation: Be your character as animal or insect

If your character were an animal or insect, what would s/he be?
What animal's or insect's rhythm
                        personality
                        sense of work or play

most closely correspond to the same characteristics
in your character?

    A fox?
    An ant?
    A lynx?
    A racehorse?
    A workhorse?

Once you have decided,
or while you are in the process of making a choice,
go to a zoo or a sanctuary or outdoors, wherever necessary,
and observe your animal or insect.

After you have observed your model
and come to terms with its rhythm, needs and style,
come back to the classroom situation.

Imagine the animal or insect is in your center.

Let it grow until it encompasses all of you.

From your stomach
   to the top of your head
     out to the tips of your fingers
       down to your toes

*transform yourself to the animal or insect so
that you can move with its rhythm.*

FEEL
THINK
ACT   LIKE THE ANIMAL
REACT

Design: Be your character as animal or insect

Transform the classroom into a wildlife sanctuary.

Lie down as your animal and go to sleep.

Now awaken

alert

ready to eat.

Run

play

work

fight

as your character's animal.

Experience your character as animal or insect for a while.

Design: Be your character as half human/half animal

Transform yourself back to your character,
but retain your animal's mind and rhythm.

Move through space for a time
in this half human/half animal state.

By retaining the animal's mentality and rhythm discover a distinguishing mentality and rhythm for your character.

In this zoological fantasy you can discover new and exciting rhythm possibilities for your character.

Anne Meacham once modeled her characterization of Hedda on her cat. The resulting Ibsen heroine was restless, dangerous, easily bored, ready to claw—easily one of the most exciting Heddas ever seen.

OBJECT

Preparation: Be your character as object

If your character's essential qualities were to be solidified into an object, what would it be?

A diamond?
An old shoe?

A toilet?
A jigsaw puzzle?
A glass of champagne?
A thunderstorm?

Make your choice.

Put that object in your center.

Let it grow until it becomes you,
until in character you have transformed yourself
into that object.

Don't aim only to change yourself
into a physical resemblance of that object.
Incorporate in your transformation
the object's *soul*.

Design: Be your character as object

Decide on an appropriate situation: a party
a factory
the city street.

Decide on an intention
appropriate to your character as object
in that situation.

SPEAK

MOVE   with the rest of the class in that situation

THINK   as though you were your object come to life.

INTERACT

Design: **Be your character as** _____

Sum up your character's essential qualities in a color

song

dance

whatever.

Put that image into your center.

Experiment and *learn* from its presence.

Adapt any of the improvisations in the chapter on improvisation to learn more about your character.

CARRYTHROUGH: AUTOBIOGRAPHY

By now you should know a lot about your character. Make it actable.

In character, write your autobiography.

Write the autobiography in h(er/is) handwriting
  on the paper s/he would use
  with the pen or pencil s/he would have
  in the form s/he would choose.

Be aware that your character may hide certain feelings about h(er/im)self from h(er/im)self.

Sum up. Make $\begin{Bmatrix} \text{concise} \\ \text{immediate} \\ \text{actable} \end{Bmatrix}$ everything your character feels about. h(er/im)self.

The point has been made that the actor must transform h(er/im)self from the inside out in order to become h(is/er) character.

S/he must walk the way the character walks,
   talk the way the character talks,
      look
      think
      breathe
      act
      react   like the character.

It sometimes happens that the process of transforming self to character is spontaneous—or so we are led to believe.
The actor is cast,
and with little work,
seemingly by some divination,
s/he becomes the role.

Most of us, though, have to work long, hard hours to produce a work of artistry. We are drones, meticulously working away from morning to night, week in and week out.

This does not mean, however, that we can never produce anything but a pale copy of the work of true artistry. The fact of the matter is that most great artists are great drones as well.

{ Marlon Brando
George C. Scott
Charlie Chaplin
Vanessa Redgrave }

like

{ Pablo Picasso
Jean-Paul Sartre
Alicia Alonso
Maria Callas }

} work at their craft.

They know what you must learn:

like painting
writing
dancing or
singing

acting = whatever
artistry
one
may
have

+ whatever
craft
one
may
have

+ weeks
months
years
of
hard
hard
work.

CARRYTHROUGH: LIFE/ART CRISSCROSS

Obviously the more you, yourself, have lived,
the more you have experienced,
the more you know and feel,
the better you will be able to transform yourself
to one character,
then another.

Know that everything you do and learn in your life
dovetails into something you can use in acting.

So continue to prepare yourself off stage
for your characterizations on stage.

Read
Get a pet
Make scrapbooks
Write letters
Fantasize
Explore painting
Go to zoos
Experience music
Keep diaries

Observe people, all kinds, in all kinds of places.
Discover them
Make contact with them
Sympathize with them
Empathize with them
Analyze them
Analyze yourself
Get to know an enemy
Love people
Love yourself

8. Emotion

All too often when an actor speaks on stage
s/he does not emotionally involve h^{er}imself
in what s/he is saying.
S/he merely mouths words.

S/he says them as though they belonged to another
and s/he is only borrowing them for the purposes of the play.
S/he will return them to the owner when the play is over
without any sign of use.
They will be as good as new.

Quite the reverse must happen.
You, the actor, must assimilate and manipulate words.

It is not enough that you *know* what you are saying;
you must also *feel* what you are saying.

This means
you must make every word you say on stage your own
and you must pay whatever emotional price that ownership demands.
Needless to say,
the more powerful the words,
the higher the price.

Use your own experience in real life as proof
of the extraordinary involvement powerful words demand.

Think of a time when someone called you
"ignorant!" or "boring!"

Recall how your face flushed
how you wanted to strike out
to humiliate the one who had humiliated you.

Conversely, think of a time when,
for your own protection,
you had to say to someone,

"Get out of my life. I can't take it anymore,"
or a phrase equally as cutting,
equally as decisive.

Remember the accumulation of hurts,
the frustrations,
the building tensions
that led to your blurting out that final invective.

Now try to recall
what happened to you physically
when you said the words.

Perhaps your eyes burned and teared.
Perhaps your voice screeched
as though coming from a lunatic
and your body trembled uncontrollably
as though in the throes of physical disease.

But the malady was not physical.
It was emotional.

The reason the physical manifestations were so convulsive
was that the emotional provocation was so total.

As in real life off stage so in theatrical life on stage:

Words demand total emotional investments

from both the one who says them

and the one who hears them.

As an actor you must be ready to make that personal, emotional investment, no matter how small or how great the claim may be.

It is not just the show of emotion that is called for, it is emotion itself.

Never, never decide
that you can rise to the occasion of emotion on stage
with only an exterior show of it.

Fist clenching, sullen stares, shouting, crying, screaming—
all such evidences of emotion mean nothing
in and of themselves.

Only if they grow out of and
        are supported by real feeling
will they matter.
Without this support
any emotional display

on stage or off
is mere bombast.

Where do you get the necessary emotional support?

From YOURSELF!

You carry around with you at all times
enough emotional power to fill most any dramatic moment six times over.
And the more you live—
the more you experience
        know
            feel—

the greater and more varied your emotional capacity.

As an actor you should look forward to growing older.
You should look forward to the fact that in your maturity
your emotional power will range from joy to rage and
include all fine gradations of emotions between these two extremes.

But no matter how vast and varied your emotional capacity is now
and no matter how much more vast and varied it will become as you mature,
it will do you no good unless you know how to tap it.

Your actor tasks, therefore, are

203

to get in touch with your own emotional resources

to learn how to tap those resources when you need them for stage use.

Preparation: Experiencing your own emotional power

The following design will make great demands on your *voice*.
Do a vocal warm-up to make certain that
your voice is ready for the demands about to be made on it.
Otherwise you could injure your voice.

Hum the notes of the scale.

Prolong each note five or six beats,
breathing when you need to.
Do not force or strain.
You are not in an endurance contest.
You are simply warming up your vocal chords by
letting warm, hummed air pass over them.

Now chew a note.

Chew it as thoroughly as you would
a mouthful of steak—tough steak.

Bring your forehead into play as you are chewing.

Use your eyes and nose also.

Chew with your entire face.

Stay HERE and NOW as you chew.

Now chew an entire sentence:
"I'm going over to Mary's for a while."
Say the sentence and chew all the while.
It's the same process as if you were trying to speak
while chewing a mouthful of taffy.

Now carry on a conversation with another class member,
each of you continuing to chew your steak or taffy
as you talk to one another.

Stay HERE and NOW.

Talk and chew.

When your voice and face feel tinglingly alive
relaxed
READY

the exercise is over.

Now get your *body* in the same state of readiness.

Stand still,
feet slightly apart so you have good support.

Now throw away your left arm.
It's almost the same process as if you were throwing a ball,
only freer.

Throw it away.
You don't need it anymore.

You don't need your right arm anymore either.
Throw it away.

What about your left leg?
You can do without it.

And throw away your right leg too.
Make it a big toss.

Last of all throw away your body.

Now throw it away again.

And again.

And once more.

Now, continuing to keep your feet slightly apart
and flat on the floor for good support,
bend your knees
but keep the rest of your body erect.

In that relaxed position
gently bounce up and down
(not vigorously, gently).

At the same time turn your body from side to side.
Your feet do not move so you do not make a complete rotation.
You simply bounce up and down
as you twist from side to side.

Hum as you perform this relaxing, readying body vibration.

Continue the exercise for a couple of minutes.
By that time, excess tension should be excised
and your body and voice should be
ready to go.

Design : Detonate!

In this design you will be given a series of powerfully evocative words and phrases by the teacher-guide. Say and experience each word/phrase until you are given the next one. The time it takes to fully experience each word/phrase will vary, but probably you will spend no less than fifteen minutes. With some extremely evocative words/phrases you might spend as long as an hour.

This design can be accomplished either with one actor experiencing a word/phrase while the rest of the class looks on or with the entire class experiencing the word/phrase at the same time. Or the teacher-guide can ask that some phrases be experienced alone, some in groups. The procedure is the same.

Find your own space.

Put yourself in the center of that space.

Establish a circle of solitude around you.

You can see out of that circle
but no one can see in.
Hence, within your space
you have total freedom to do what you want.
No prying eyes can invade your sanctuary
as you set about discovering
the emotional levels of your own being.

If all the class is working at the same time,
you might hear the phrases of others as they say them.
Feed off their power,
but do not allow their experience to interfere with yours.
Concentrate on your own experience
and no one else need disturb you.

Once you are in your own space

with your circle of solitude drawn around you,

you are ready to begin the design.

The teacher-guide will give you a word or phrase, such as

"Who do you think you are!"

Earn your right to say that phrase:

Close your eyes.

Recall a time when you said that phrase to someone,
or just as important,
wished you had said it.

See the situation of your provocation precisely.
See every detail of the setting.
Feel any textures you felt at the time.
Smell any odors you smelled at the time.
Hear any sounds you heard at the time.

Above all
see the person to whom you were speaking.
See him very exactly.

You, a woman, see a man who has humiliated you.
See his clothing
his stance
his expression.
Remember the tone of his voice.
Remember *everything* about him—

every detail of the way he looked
and acted in that situation.

A point should be elaborated on. The situation you are creating
need not actually have happened to you. You may have wished
it had happened.

At a particular time in your past you might have been
insulted by an authority figure—a boss, a teacher, a mother.
At that time you wanted to say, "Who do you think you are!"
but you were afraid of offending that person, perhaps for
fear of what s/he could do to you in reprisal. You said
nothing. You may now re-create that kind of situation in
which you wanted to confront someone, in which you
wanted to throw someone's rudeness, cruelty, or
indifference back in his/her face, but did not.

After you have re-created the situation—
real or imaginary—
once you *see* it and *feel* it,
let it pull from you the phrase.

See each new situation clearly.
Exactly.
See the person.
Let each new situation act as a stimulus for your phrase.

If the entire class is realizing and experiencing the word/phrase at the same time, you may discover that no matter how involved you are or how hard you concentrate, you are being pulled out of your own experience by the force of someone else's voice. In this event, use a variation of the HERE and NOW exercise to pull yourself back into the center of your own experience.

In the HERE and NOW exercise
you were asked to examine very closely
things in your real, immediate environment
in order to keep your consciousness
in present time.

In this variation
you should reexamine very closely
the elements of your imagined environment
in order to keep your consciousness
in this situation.

After you have exhausted your responses to situations provoked by the phrase, the teacher-guide will give you other words/phrases. Make certain you follow the design instructions for each new word/phrase:

Find your own space.

Draw a *circle of solitude* around yourself.

Listen to the phrase.

Earn your right to say it by
re-creating a situation in which
you said
or wished you had said
the phrase.

See every detail of that situation
so that you relive
and reexperience it.

Then say the word/phrase.

Other emotionally evocative words/phrases:

Mother (or whatever you call your mother)

Father (or whatever you call your father)

Wow

I love you

I hate you

Oh, yeah?

I like it

No

Yes

Why not

Don't leave me

Get out of here

Never again

I'll do it

Leave me alone

It's beautiful

Let's go swimming

The name of someone you love or
                have loved or
                can't love no matter how hard you try

If you truly persevere in these individual word/phrase
experiences, you can discover emotional powder kegs that will
be as thrilling as they are useful to you as an actor. But,
however exciting these experiences may be, they are exhausting.
After completing two or three experiences take a break by
doing the following design.
It can clear your mind
        relax your body and
        let you have a little fun.

Lie down on the floor.

Close your eyes.

You are floating on a cloud.
It is the softest, most billowy cloud ever.
You never thought you would see the day
when you would float on a cloud,
to say nothing of floating on such a wonderful cloud.
What a great surprise!

Feel the cloud all around you.

Feel it in your nose
    in your eyes
        in your teeth.

It feels marvelous
It smells marvelous.
Take a bite of it.
It tastes marvelous too!

Now the cloud is moving,
wafting you around the sky.

You have become weightless.
When you lift your arm or your leg
it floats up.

No exertion required;
the cloud supports you.

Now open your eyes.
Not only are you floating on a cloud
which was fun enough
but everyone else in the class is here with you.
What a doubly marvelous surprise!

Stand up.
Move on the cloud.
Play.
You can touch one another.
Have fun with one another.
You can even roll and toss and rise and fall with one another.
There is no need to worry.
The cloud will support you.
Everything is easy, light, free, and fun.

Now lie down on the cloud again.
Stretch out on it.
Roll over on it.
Feel it soft on your chest.
Make cloud noises.
Sigh or sing to the cloud.

Troll
Chant
Warble } to the cloud.
Yodel
Whistle

Your voice is as free and easy and supported by the cloud as everything and everyone about you.

Now the cloud starts to tickle your feet.

Now it tickles you in the ribs.

Now it stops tickling.

You lie there for a second more

so f r e   e

so relaxed

so ready.

Go back to the emotionally evocative word/phrase.

Experience each fully.

Go to the limit.

Hold nothing back.

After experiencing a single word/phrase, sit in a circle and discuss what happened to you. The discussion will prove most useful to all if, one by one, you describe in exact detail the situations that provoked you to respond with your word.

One boy
described in the following way a
situation that provoked his calling
out the word "Mother":

"I was eight years old.
It was late at night.
I was alone in my room
trying to get to sleep.
The lights were out, but
a ray of light spilled into my room
from the hallway.
I could see the figure
of a large man in the shadows.
I heard a strange noise.
I was so afraid

I dared not speak or move.
Finally
I got up the courage to call my mother.
I called to her again and again
until she came to see what was wrong."

In describing these situations in such exact detail, you are doing
nothing less than constructing a means to put yourself in touch
with and in command of your own emotional resources.

Through the power of imagination
you create or re-create
an emotionally evocative situation.

The imaginary actor-created situation
evokes from you
a real response.

In the preceding description
the eight-year-old child
alone in his bedroom
was imagined
but the fear evoked and
the consequent call to "Mother"
were real.

If in the future

this actor needs to feel fear on stage—and
the immediate circumstances of the stage
situation don't pull from him the desired
emotional response—
he can see in his mind's eye
the dark scary room of his childhood
and the emotion will come.

In describing what happens to you in these emotionally
evocative situations you should also discover that you have
been using another principle of acting applicable to virtually any
acting situation:

In your real response to this imaginary situation you played an intention:

You spoke to a person
to get h^{er}_{im} to feel a particular way
so s/he would do the desired act.

The eight-year-old called to "Mother"
so she would feel sorry for him
and come to his side to comfort him.

A final discovery you should make is that without consciously
deciding what to do physically in each of these situations, you
probably behaved appropriately.

The point here is that
if your emotional provocation
is real and felt,
your body will respond
in an appropriate and dramatic manner.

An interesting classroom assignment can
grow out of this design:

Each person can prepare one (or however many)
of the situations s/he created when s/he
was earning h_{is}^{er} right to say h_{is}^{er} word/phrase.

In the instance of the frightened eight-year-old, the
actor could "become" himself when he was eight
and enact all the events that led up to his calling,
"Mother." He could also, should he choose, select
another member of the class to play his mother. In
assigning another actor the role of his mother, the
actor must take care to describe his mother in detail
so that his partner will understand the character
she is to portray.

The scene should be prepared
and then presented to the class.

Carrythrough

Prove to yourself the extraordinary range of your emotional repertoire. Jot down in your workbook all the emotional changes you experience in just one day.

Suggested format:

Start with the state of feeling you are in when you get up in the morning.

Jot down the motivation for your first change of emotion.

This motivation can be something that happened to you or something you imagined. Our imaginings cause as many and almost as severe emotional changes as do events that happen to us in the real world.

Jot down your new state of feeling.

Continue this format for the entire day: state of feeling

motivation for
change of feeling

new state of feeling

Another valuable carrythrough is to observe other people when they are in the grip of an emotion.

Watch how their bodies move.

Tune into their rhythm.

Listen to their voices.

Go home and re-create the observed experience.

In re-creating the observed experience you might want to "substitute" an emotional provocation of your own for the one you observed. Say you saw and overheard a woman on the telephone crying as she talked to a friend about a job loss. When you become the woman of the observed scene, think of something in your own life that made you cry. Then keep your personal emotionally evocative event in your consciousness as you enact that woman in her scene. In other words substitute your own experience for hers so that your emotional response will be real.

Carrythrough with script

Ask the question:
WHAT MATTERS MOST TO YOUR CHARACTER?

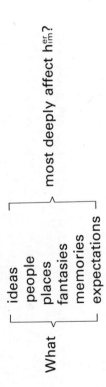

What
ideas
people
places
fantasies
memories
expectations
most deeply affect h$_{im}^{er}$?

To answer the question look to the play,
paying particular attention, first of all,
to *what the character says about h$_{im}^{er}$self.*

Specifically look for times when the character says I want
I need
I long for
(or the equivalent).

In *No Exit*
Garcin says to Estelle:

"If there's someone, just one person,
to say quite positively I did not run away,

that I'm not the sort who runs away,
that I'm brave and decent and the rest of it—
well, that one person's faith would save me.
Will you have that faith in me? . . .
If you'll have faith in me I'm saved."

Also pay attention to *what other characters say about* him.[er.]

In *The Way of the World*
Fainall says about Lady Wishfort:

"I believe the lady will do anything to get a husband."

In *Joe Egg*
Sheila talks about her husband to the audience:

"I'm sure, though, if he could go farther—
he could be a marvellous painter . . .
And even if he *isn't* any good,
he seems to need some work he can be proud of."

Also look for *dialogues in which
characters passionately reveal their need to one another.*

In *Summer and Smoke*:

JOHN   I've settled with life on fairly acceptable terms. Isn't that all a reasonable person can ask for?

ALMA   He can ask for much more than that.
        He can ask for the coming true of his most improbable dreams.

JOHN   It's best not to ask for too much.

In *Yerma*:

JUAN   Without children life is sweet. I am happy not having them . . .

YERMA   Then what do you want with me?

JUAN   Yourself!

YERMA   . . . even when you knew I wanted [a child]?

But don't accept anything anyone says at face value. Either the character himself or the person talking about him could be lying.

You have to weigh all the evidence and then decide.
Pay particular attention to what characters do.
Look to their action.
Then compare and contrast their action with their words.

In *Hamlet* Rozencrantz and Guildenstern
profess themselves to be great friends of Hamlet;
their action proves that the reverse is true.

In analyzing the character's action
look to see if there is any action s/he does compulsively.
Such an action will tell you the most significant things
about that character.

In *A Streetcar Named Desire*
Blanche covers the glaring light bulb with a chinese lantern,
soaks herself in a tub for hours, and
dresses herself in faded elegance—

    revealing her need for beauty
    in a mechanized world.

In *The Glass Menagerie*
Laura repeatedly steals off to polish and admire
her glass animals—

    finding there
    the solace and delicacy she needs.

In *Blood Wedding*
Leonardo races his horse night after night—

      sublimating his intense sexual need
        for the woman he loves.

After you have examined your character in all h[er]is revelations in the play
and have determined the people and ideas that obsess h[er]im,

transform yourself to character

find your space

draw around yourself a

circle of solitude

Choose an emotionally evocative word.

Earn your right to say the word by
seeing a person or a situation
that acts as a stimulation
pulling the word from you.

If you are playing Lorca's barren Yerma
whose sole reason for being is to have a baby:

Transform yourself to character.

Close your eyes.

Say the words "my baby" over and over again.

Images that might flash into your mind:

your own baby
as s/he might look

spinsters
whose barren state haunts you

your husband
who will not give you a baby

Victor the shepherd
who could give you a baby

faces of outcast women
who defy society and live as they choose

friends
with children of their own

After you have exhausted your responses to this phrase
choose another from the text or subtext of the play and
let it pull a range of responses from you.

In this way, *discover*

come to terms with } the emotions of your character.

live

9. IMPROVISATION

On stage everything must seem to happen for the first time.

Everything must look fresh
      extemporaneous
      new
      NOW.

It is the actor who is responsible for this improvisatory attitude:
it is s/he who must act and react as if everything that is happening
on stage were happening for the first time.

But the question is, after weeks of rehearsing
                                    memorizing
                                    polishing
                                    refining her/his work on character and play,

how does the actor make her/his life on stage seem improvised?

The only sure way to master the improvisatory attitude is to *improvise*.

In improvisation the actor explores the nature of the situation
    and this leads her/him to true feelings on stage.

In improvisation the actor cannot follow preconceived,
    conventional patterns of behavior
    because there aren't any.

In improvisation things look extemporaneous
    because they are.

In improvisation the actor has to rely on her/his own will
                                            intelligence
                                            emotion
                                            ingenuity

    because that's all s/he has.

In improvisation the actor has to play the NOW
    because that's all there is.

Enter each of the following improvisations ready to
discover the improvisatory attitude and to
keep it through every moment
of your work on stage
        in rehearsed plays
                before an audience.

PREPARATION: WARM-UP

Do a thorough vocal and physical warm-up (see pages 4–6, 319–320).

Then
run around the room four times.

You're ready.   Set.   Begin.

PLAYING GAMES

The objectives in playing games are to develop

    group spirit

    imagination

respect for rules of the game

a sense of serious fun (each player plays as if
everything depended on his playing well)

concentration (if each player doesn't concentrate
every moment in a game, s/he is likely to lose)

natural, coordinated, organic use of body and voice

free, rhythmical breathing
while performing difficult physical tasks

the habit of focusing attention
on goals through and beyond movement

real $\left\{\begin{array}{c} \text{living} \\ \text{thinking} \\ \text{feeling} \end{array}\right\}$ on stage

playing the NOW of existence

**The objectives of games
are objectives of acting.**

Tug of war

Divide the players into two teams.

Each team lines up, one player behind the other.

Each player puts h$^{er}_{is}$ arms around the person in front of h$^{er}_{im}$.

Draw a line between the two teams, separating them.

The lead person of each team pulls the other's arms, trying to pull the opposing team across the line.

Once that happens, the game is over.

Go on to another.

Kelly says

The leader of a group instructs the players in the group to do what Kelly says and nothing else.

    If Kelly says
    jump up and down,
    jump up and down;

237

if Kelly says
sing like Marlene Dietrich,
sing like Marlene Dietrich.

The object is for Kelly to trick a player
into following a simple direction unpreceded by the words "Kelly says."

The loser then becomes the leader
and the game starts all over again.

Hide and seek

The person who is "it" locates him(er)self at home base and then
closes his(er) eyes and counts a slow fifteen or a fast thirty,
giving the rest of the players a chance to hide.

When "it" reaches the full count s/he opens his(er) eyes and
attempts to find each player before s/he is able to reach home base.

Tag

The person who is "it" tries to tag someone else
who then becomes "it."

Variations:

tag in slow motion

tag on one foot

swat tag (a person with a newspaper is "it,"
swats another with the paper, and
passes the paper on to the new "it")

Follow the leader

All the players line up behind a leader
who does an action—body rolls
convulsive shaking
sniffing and searching.

All players repeat this action.

After a time, someone else becomes the leader and
initiates the action.

Variation: Try this to music and dance to the leader.

Make me laugh

Someone stands in the center of a group and
tries to make the others break up laughing
by telling jokes, making funny faces, making innuendoes, and so on.

239

The first person who laughs assumes the role of laugh provoker.

Musical chairs

Set up a row of chairs having one less chair than the number of players.

Move in a circle around the row of chairs to music and continue to do so until the music stops.

Try to sit in an empty chair.

The player who cannot find a seat is the loser of that round and is excluded from the rest of the game.

Remove another chair, resume the music, and go round again.

Repeat until there is only one chair and two players.

The player who doesn't get that chair loses the game.

Red Rover

Two teams line up facing each other, arms linked so as to form a human fortress.

One team designates a member of the other team to come over by saying, "Red Rover
Red Rover
Send Mary right over."

Mary's challenge is to break through the barrier line.

If Mary fails to break through
she becomes a member of the opposing team.

If she succeeds
she takes a player of the opposing team back to her team.

This continues until one team is playerless.

Blind man's buff

All players locate themselves in a space.

One player is blindfolded and twirled round and round until s/he has lost his sense of where s/he is and where everyone else is.

The blindfolded person now tries to tag another player.

Each player is duty bound to keep one foot in the space
where s/he began the experience.
But s/he can move the rest of h$^{er}_{is}$ body as much as s/he chooses.

When the blind man tags someone
that person is then blindfolded
and the game begins again.

Carrythrough

Play as many of these games as you wish.

Then
each class member think of a game or two from h$^{er}_{is}$ childhood.
Teach it to the rest of the class and
play it.

DEVELOPING TRUST AND UNDERSTANDING

Yield

Find a partner.

S/he will close h$^{er}_{is}$ eyes
making h$^{er}_{im}$ totally dependent on you.

Responding to the trust given you
take your partner's hand and
guide h$^{er}_{im}$ through a series of nonthreatening
                diverse
                evocative   experiences.

Because your partner has been cut off from h$^{er}_{is}$ sense of sight
the experience may well awaken and enhance h$^{er}_{is}$ sense of touch
                                    smell
                                    taste
                                    hearing.

Sensual things you might try:

Glide your partner's hand over multiplaned
                    variously shaped surfaces.

Give h$^{er}_{im}$ a sip of water.

Make tiny musical noises in h$^{er}_{is}$ ear.

Lead h$^{er}_{im}$ to different temperature experiences: an open window
                                        a heat vent.

243

Guide h_{er}im (gently) up and down stairs

ramps

levels.

If it is warm outside,
take off h_{er}is shoes and
lead h_{er}im outdoors to grass and trees and fresh air.
Let h_{er}im experience the touch and smell and taste of nature.

After an hour or so,
change roles.

S/he will guide,
you will follow and experience.

Don't lose body contact with your partner during this time of h_{er}is
blind dependence on you.

Make the experience as pleasant as possible.

Allow your partner sufficient—but not overly much—time to
explore each experience before you lead h_{er}im to the next.

Vary the experiences and be creative in your offerings.

Names

Find a partner.

Stand back to back.

Link arms.

Feed off one another's movement impulses
as you gently sway or rock or bend together.

As you move together
say your partner's name over and over again
as s/he says yours.

Sometimes whisper it.
Sometimes sing it.
Sometimes shout it.
Sometimes laugh it.

_____ Develop an alternating routine of saying the names: you say his/her
name, then s/he'll say yours.

_____ Don't move in such a way that your partner will be
uncomfortable.

245

Vary intentions as you use your partner's name:
alternately try to amuse
  frighten
  win
  cajole h$_{im}^{er}$.

Find one another

Close your eyes.

Gently twirl yourself in space
till you forget where you are and
    who is next to you.

Call to another player and try to find h$_{im}^{er}$.
(Don't open your eyes to seek h$_{im}^{er}$ out,
but use all the other senses.)

When you find h$_{im}^{er}$,
give h$_{im}^{er}$ a kiss on the nose.

Then call to another actor
find h$_{im}^{er}$
kiss h$_{im}^{er}$
until you have found and nose-kissed everyone in the room.

At the same time as you are calling a name
someone may be calling yours.
If you hear your name being called
make your way toward the source
so you can get your kiss on the nose.

_____ You will touch and be touched a lot in this game. Enjoy it.

_____ Call softly enough so everyone can hear one another in the
jumble of names.

_____ Keep your eyes closed so all other senses will open extra wide.

Symbiosis

Divide up into groups of four.

Start to move in
         out
         over
         around one another.

In your movement explore all possible planes
                                         levels
                                         body positions.

247

Always stay in body contact with as many of the quartet as you can.

Develop in your moving relationship a bond of trust and respect for your fellow actors as you sometimes slide under them sometimes roll over them as they in turn are gliding

rolling over

and

under

and

around you

This experience asks all players to develop a keen awareness of one another. For many times in the movement you and the other actors will be in very vulnerable positions.

All must be protected.

Develop a sixth sense
that keeps you aware of and
responsive to the position and
needs of your fellow actors.

Be and breathe together

Lie down on your side
in a relaxed, comfortable position.
Fall into an easy breathing pattern.

Another actor lies down behind you,
snuggling up next to you,
his body touching the full length of yours.

Let your rhythms mesh
until you are breathing as one organism.

Another actor lies down and breathes as one with you
and another
and another
all of you forming one organism.

Do something nice

Embrace in friendship

249

Give a gift (it doesn't have to be real; imaginary ones are just as much fun)

Give a body massage

Receive a body massage

DEVELOPING A SENSE OF SCENE DYNAMICS: FROM HERE →→ TO →→ THERE

The next improvisations involve scene work.

Here is a list of improvisatory situations for one person

two people

groups of people.

One-person situations

a dream
a fantasy

preparing for a date
party
exam
interview
a telephone conversation

saying a poem to your dog
    in a shower
        on a beach
           to a machine

doing a task: waiting
           painting
           sewing
           drinking
           cleaning
           exercising

waking up in the morning; at midday
being born
dying

Two-person situations

date (blind or otherwise)
roommates in their room or elsewhere
audition
waiting for the results of an exam to be posted
first to arrive at a party
           funeral
              shower
                class

cabal
job interview
country club
laundromat
bowling alley
salesperson/customer
librarian/book seeker

Group situations

union meeting
classroom
theatre lobby
picnic
street fair
birthday party
rainstorm
last (or first) day of class
sporting event
barn raising
dance
television studio
movie
bus ⎤
train ⎬ station
plane ⎦

Available material

"Dear Abby" letters
jokes
newspaper items
paintings (Manet's *Picnic on the Grass*)
historical incidents
songs
poems

For each of the following improvisations,
choose an improvisatory situation from this list
or make up one of your own
or use the one suggested (if it is!)
or use an already scripted scene.

Realize its dynamics:
play the scene
so that it goes
from HERE ⟶ to ⟶ THERE.

Environment

Choose an improvisatory scene.

253

Play the scene as though the environmental conditions
were the principal factor to be reckoned with:

> It is dark
> > wet
> > windy
> > the first day of spring
> > dusty
> > muddy

What's happening off stage

Play a scene as though you were being overheard
and you do
or do not
want to be.

How long will this go on!

Play a scene as though the wrecker were coming in five minutes
and everything—
absolutely everything—
will be torn down.

Play a scene as if you were going to be in this exact place
with this exact person
for a long, l o n g time.

Rhythm

Play a scene to clapped rhythms
(the teacher-guide or another actor can provide the rhythm).

Play the scene as if you had to go to the bathroom—NOW
　　you were high (or low) on (choose a drug or alcohol)
　　you were dead tired
　　you were dead
　　you were underwater
　　you were naked
　　the other person were pointing a knife at you.

Play the scene to the accompaniment of different musical rhythms:

　　Scott Joplin ragtime
　　Miles Davis jazz
　　Charlie Byrd bossanova
　　Leadbelly blues
　　John Philip Sousa march

Intensity

Play the same dynamic with your partner.

Start the scene: *As the scene progresses
                            you steadily become:*

angry   angrier and angrier
bored   more and more bored
wet ——→ drier
young   older
sexy   sexier

In the following scenes you and your partner may have either the same or a conflicting dynamic.

Start the scene: *As the scene progresses:*

adventuresome   you both become more and more adventuresome
comfortable ——→ you become warmer; s/he gets colder
sexy   you become sexier; s/he becomes sadder

It's not the words, it's what you do with them

Play the following dialogue:

A   Hi

B   Hello

A   Home early today

B   Not so early

A   Early enough

B   For what

A   I don't know

B   I do

in different situations:

A man is talking to his parents
after just having found out his wife is unfaithful.

A child arrives home after winning an award
after being kicked out of school.

Two friends are in a quarrel
are making up after a quarrel.

An insurance salesperson is talking to a prospective client.

Former $\left\{\begin{array}{l}\text{lovers}\\\text{friends}\\\text{enemies}\end{array}\right.$ meet after a four-year separation.

Move the audience

By directly or indirectly playing h$^{er}_{is}$ intention,
one person moves a crowd to feel silly

sad
angry
defeated
formal
adventuresome
resentful
confused.

The rest of the class becomes the audience.

It's best if the audience imagines themselves as children. Children say and do what they feel; they go as the spirit moves them.

Two people perform a scene intending
to move the audience to respond in a particular way.

Play the scene so that the audience will clap
                                        laugh
                                        boo
                                        hiss
                                        walk away
                                        turn their backs
                                        get under the chairs
                                        play with you
                                        play among themselves
                                        yell "Get the hook!"
                                             "Watch out!"

Play it for laughs

Build a scene to a sight gag:

    a pratfall
    a double take
    a pie in the face
    a sleight-of-hand trick

We never know what will happen

Preparation

Alone in your room
get ready to go on a date
    take an exam
    have a talk with an enemy
        with a friend

    get married or
    get divorced.

Before you begin the scene
decide your attitude toward the forthcoming event, and
let that state of feeling inform you as you are getting ready.

You dread having to talk with your friend
because you have disappointed him/her.

Surprise

When you have completed getting yourself ready for the event
the teacher-guide will tell you what actually happened.
This may be quite different from what you thought would happen.

When you were getting ready you dreaded talking with your friend,
fearful that s/he would be angry with you.
But as it turned out s/he wasn't angry, s/he was pleased.
Or s/he was angrier than you had thought.

Postscript

Go home.
Get ready for bed
letting your new state of feeling inform you.

Character swap tag

During a small group scene any character may tag another
and the two characters then swap roles.

Sample situation: a party.

Each class member
assumes a very definite character: leach
                                     drunk
                                     jock
                                     boring and continuous storyteller
                                     center of the party

It may be helpful for the player who is planning to swap roles
with another to warn him a minute or so before actually tagging.

261

____ The requirements are definite, projectable character creation and careful continuous observation of every other character in the scene at all times.

Secret aversion and attraction

Find a partner.

Together, decide roles and situation.

Susan and Julie are students and close friends. Susan goes to Julie's room to borrow a record. While there, Julie offers Susan some cake.

Privately decide on the particular aversion and attraction each has for the other person.

Susan likes Julie's generous spirit but can't stand to be around Julie when she eats because she eats like a pig.

Julie likes Susan's company but dislikes Susan's propensity to borrow and not return things.

Neither one of you is to have any idea what the other thinks of you. What you think about the person (and what she thinks about you) may not be true; the important thing is that each of you feels it to be true.

Play the scene
without verbalizing either your aversion or attraction, but allow the attitudes to influence your actions.

I want it/You want it

Build a scene around a mutual desire to acquire an object.

Set a ball down on the floor.
Two characters enter.
Both want the ball.
One is going to get it.

You cannot just run over to the ball and take it. (Your motivation: other people might be looking and besides, s/he might be faster.)

In the course of the scene you must establish
who you are
where you are
what the importance of the object is to you.

Homilies

Divide into groups of three.
Each group will be given the same homily to dramatize:

>Better safe than sorry
>The early bird catches the worm
>A stitch in time saves nine

After five minutes of preparation,
each group enacts its rendition for the rest.

>Never use the phrase itself.
>Your interpretation may be literal
>   surreal
>   expressionistic.

_____

>The sky's the limit
>(and a little beyond).

Compatible and incompatible objectives

Divide the class in half.

Group A is given an objective,
Group B another (or the same one).

Neither knows the other's objective.

Group A is told in private that
they want to get Group B to help clean the room.

Group B is told they want to get out of the room.

Never state your intention. Instead, play it subtly, persuasively,
as you try to get the other group to feel a particular way so they
will do the desired thing.

In the scene you can play in whatever groupings you choose: one to one
one to three
two to four.

_____

Get the other guy to take the responsibility

After mutually agreeing to go someplace,
change your mind.

Get the other person to renege
so you don't have to reveal why you don't want to go.

Because: | *get the other person to say:*

you're afraid of rides | s/he doesn't want to go to the carnival

you'll get saddle sores | s/he doesn't want to go horseback riding

you're an acrophobiac | s/he doesn't want to go to the top of the Empire State Building

you're on a diet | s/he doesn't want a big meal

you have poison ivy | s/he doesn't want to consummate the relationship

Change in plans

Play a scene involving a change in plans.

Plan | *Change in plan*

People on a vacation cruiser having a good time | suddenly are informed a hurricane is approaching.

People in a museum absorbed in looking, studying	discover they are locked in.
People on a train	feel the train stop.

ADVANCING THE PLOT

Carry the action forward

One actor starts an action.

Other actors observe h$^{er}_{im}$ until they perceive what the task is.

One at a time they enter the scene
contribute to the task
bring it to completion.

The entering actor cannot do the same activity as was initiated by the first actor. Each adds to the action but does not duplicate it.

Actor A enters	paints a wall with a roller
Actor B enters	does the detail work with a brush

Actor C enters — mixes paint and pours it into
containers when they are empty

Actors D and E enter — bring coffee and rolls and give
the two painters a break

Actors A and B — resume painting and bring it to
completion

Carrythrough

Always when you are in a play
add to the action when you enter the scene
establish how your character advances the plot and
give focus to the main activity.

Solution/Resolution

Two people are involved in an action:

a lover's quarrel

Another person enters with a
seemingly incompatible objective:

to find his dog

Resolve the scene.

The dog appears and
jumps on the woman's lap.
She and her lover start to play with it and
forget their quarrel.
The man goes off happily with his dog.

Carrythrough

Always when you are in a play
add to the action when you enter the scene
establish how your character advances the plot and
give focus to the main activity.

DREAMING AND FANTASIZING

Dreams

When you awaken in the morning
immediately jot down all you remember of your nighttime dream.
Make every detail specific—
as specific as it was in your dream.

Put yourself in the center of your dream experiences and use other actors or your own imagination for the remaining dream elements.

Now *relive* that dream
as totally as your subconscious lived it when you were sleeping.

Prepare this scene outside of class.
Bring it in.
Enact it for the teacher–guide and the class.
Get criticisms.
Take it out and rework it.
Bring it back in.

Carrythrough

Keep a diary of your dreams.
Come to grips with your creative subconscious so you can make use of it.

Fantasies

Jot down the details of your fantasies and daydreams, particularly those that recur.

Use any of these fantasies as the basis for a scene:
Put yourself in the center of your fantasies and
use other actors and/or your imagination
to supply the remaining phantasmagoric elements.

Relive the fantasy
as totally as you lived it while you were walking down the street
                alone in your room
                making love
                in the the bathtub
                mind-wandering during a lecture
                       or
                       conversation
                       or _____

Carrythrough

Keep a record of your fantasies.
Come to terms with your personal subtext
so you can make use of it.

271

Personal experiences

Write down in exact detail personal experiences of joy

trauma
boredom
sadness
excitement
sensuality.

Use any of these experiences for the basis of a scene.
Relive your personal experience as totally as you lived it at the time.

Don't forget to include childhood experiences.

Carrythrough

Keep a diary of momentous scenes in your life.
Come to terms with yourself
so you can make use of yourself.

Group fantasy

Divide into groups of five or six.

Lie down in a circle,
heads touching.

One person starts telling a fantasy.
Go around the circle.
Each person add something to it.

First person: Oh my god, what's that!
Second person: Don't go any closer.
Third person: Look out. You'll get burned.
Fourth person: It's like nothing I've ever seen.
Fifth person: Well, we're seeing it now. Only I wish I weren't.
Sixth person: Is it a dinosaur, do you think?
First person: No, don't you see, up there on its head?
There's a metal covering.

As you create the fantasy
don't describe it.
Be in the center of it.

Don't keep your fantasy earthbound.
Go anywhere.
Become anything.
Do anything.
There are no limits to imagination.

273

Let this experience go on for a full hour—
and on and on to your imagination's limit
(and then some).

After you have experienced the fantasy in your
imaginations get up as a group and enact it.

Don't contradict each other
in your group creation.

Go with
Feed off   } the group mind.
Contribute to

DEVELOPING A REPERTOIRE OF CHARACTERS

Study characters and people

Study a character in a novel
                    sculpture
                    painting
                    comic book
                    Dear Abby letter
                    advertisement   { beautiful people
                                      distressed people

or observe a person on the street.

In addition to your experiential observation ask and answer the following questions about that person:

Who am I?

What is my occupation and my attitude toward it?

How old am I?

What is my state of health?

Who were my parents?

What was my childhood like?

What ideas and people do I dislike or hate?

What ideas and people do I like or love?

What is my driving ambition—if any?

What do I like and dislike about myself?

What is my physique?

What is my center—
what is the most sensitive, expressive part of my body?

What part of the body do I lead from when I move?

What makes me sad
happy?

What physical and vocal mannerisms do I have?

How do I think other people view me?

How does this view differ from the view I have of myself?

How do I deal with conflict?

After you have asked
answered
come to terms with whichever questions seem relevant
find a partner who has similarly chosen and prepared a character.

Select an improvisatory situation suitable for your characters.

Transform yourselves to character.

Prepare the scene outside of class.
Bring it in.
Do it for the teacher–guide and the rest of the class.
Get criticisms.

Take the scene out of class and
with your added insights
rehearse the scene until you feel you both are ready to
perform once again before the class.

Carrythrough

An early drama teacher of Laurence Olivier told him to study
the people in Dickens and he'd never want for a model for
any character he would have to create on stage. Olivier
listened well and heeded the advice.

You too should do as Olivier.
In your workbook keep a diary of characters you meet in novels
on the streets
at parties
anywhere.

Have them ready for future use.

Olivier said he sometimes kept character ideas in his mind
for as long as thirteen years before he found occasion to
use them.

The point is he had them there for use when he needed them.
So should you.

Project your character

Find a partner.

Put yourselves in a neutral situation: eating potato chips
                                       on a bus
                                       browsing in a bookstore.

You want the other person to think you are a great lover
                                                    thinker
                                                    dancer
                                                    skater
                                                    singer.

You never say this about yourself
but by the way you behave
you want the other person to think it and say it.

This must be subtle; you must hint, not state (just as you yourself would do in a similar situation).

Reveal character through professional role or fantasy

As actor
let a profession or fantasy dictate your behavior.

As character
be unaware this is happening.

Professional role:

You are a typist from nine to five.
After hours your rhythm and body movement reveal that you are still possessed by your keyboard.
You have a fast rat-tat-tat way of walking and talking.
For no apparent reason, your fingers fly as if they were on keys.
(Think of Charlie Chaplin in *Modern Times* leaving the machine but acting and moving as though he were still at the machine.)

Fantasy:

You have just seen a John Wayne movie.
You have empathized and identified to the hilt with the big western he-man.

You go to work the next morning.
Unconsciously you have adapted and are enacting
some of Wayne's mannerism:

You pull out a chair to sit down, but
instead of sitting on it in the normal way
you turn it around in a strong gesture
and sit facing the back,
straddling it as though you were on a horse.

As actor
you are conscious of emulating John Wayne.
As character
you are unconscious of it.
The imitation must seem to happen
without your being aware of it.

Carrythrough

When Richard Kiley created Don Quixote and Cervantes for *Man of La Mancha*
he studied the whole play and knew
how his characterization affected the plot development
and how the plot development affected his characterization:

"I try to effect this change of attitude during the course of the play, so that Cervantes leaves the prison a different man from the one who entered."

He used paintings:

"I thought of El Greco's saints. Big men, but elongated, as in a fun-house mirror . . . . El Greco's paintings have wonderful eyes too, large, luminous, and ecstatic, seeing things the rest of us can't see."

He used novels:

"I also recalled the White Knight in *Alice in Wonderland.* His hair was stuck up in funny spikes in a way I like."

He used observation of other people:

"Old men's hands are compressed (rather than spread open). Veins and bony knuckles can be created with make-up."

He researched the novel before he began work on the play:

"I tried to get a hollow sound in my voice for Quixote . . .
I think the idea came from a line
in both the book and the play:

'This one [referring to Quixote]
has empty rooms in his head.' "

He kept a notebook in which he detailed using other actors
as models for his character's behavior.

" . . . in playing a scene as Quixote,
visualize it as being played quite nobly and legitimately
by, say, Sir Laurence Olivier."

He drew all his ideas about the character together
and sketched a portrait of Don Quixote
on the plywood floor of the stage during rehearsals.

He summed up all the character work by saying:

"I have a crazy theory
that any guy knows how to play any part and
that talent is largely a matter of getting one's self out of the way
and letting the character speak."

In the specific event of developing a character for a play

DO AS KILEY DID.

Use any or all of the improvisatory approaches described thus far.

DEVELOPING STYLE

Stendhal said:

"Style consists in adding to a given thought
all the circumstances calculated to produce the whole effect
that the thought ought to produce."

Freely adapting Stendhal's classic definition,
you will now add to a given thought sets of circumstances
in order to produce desired effects.

As if it were _____

Take the scene on pages 86–90 of "Body Acting Centers"
or write one of your own
or take one from a play.

Perform the scene as it would be performed
were it in one of the following plays
films or
television dramas:

Hair
The School of Scandal
Dracula
As the World Turns
Laugh-In
West Side Story
All in the Family
The Lucy Show
Hospital
A Night at the Opera
Ghosts
Bonanza

To do this improvisation well,
first acquaint yourselves
with the style
        tone
        manner
        stuff
of whatever play, movie, or television drama
you decide to do.

Experience firsthand—
and again and again—
the shows available to you.
Study them.
Analyze them.
Dissect them.
Come to terms with them
during and after the experience.

Use the tools in "Search and Research"
both to provide the necessary information
when direct experience is not available
and
to supplement your experiential learning.

The movie game

Ready:

Make a list of all the types of movies you know:

gangster film
World War II film
monster film
jungle film

Busby Berkeley musical
epic film
beach party film
suspense film
hospital film

Set:

Reacquaint yourself with the style
    sense
    stuff of these movies.

Go:

One of the actors in the class goes on stage
and puts him$_{er}$self in the center of one of these movies
and behaves accordingly.

In a suspense film à la Barbara Stanwyck
a girl goes center stage
stops short
listens
goes to check door
—it's locked—
starts back
hears something else

runs to check window
—it's open—
closes window
locks it
pulls the shade
starts to dial the phone
—it's dead!

After the first movie has "played" awhile
another actor enters the scene and *immediately*
by his body
words
tone
intention transforms it into another movie.

The original actor
just as immediately
transforms out of the film s/he began
into the new one beginning

Just as the girl is discovering that the phone is dead
a jungle call is heard.
Tarzan leaps on stage
calling, "I'm home, Jane."
Barbara Stanwyck now becomes Jane and says,
"You were gone so long, Tarzan; I was worried,"

and the two continue the Tarzan film:
Jane: "Where's Boy?"
Tarzan: "Isn't he with you?"

until another actor enters the scene and immediately
transforms this film to another film.

And so on.

When you enter the action
you must "take stage" immediately.
By your tone
    manner
        style
            intention
you must get everyone's attention and
communicate the movie that is now beginning
so they can understand it
and play it.

If you are beginning a Cagney gangster
film you might elect to come on stage
saying, "All right, up against the wall."

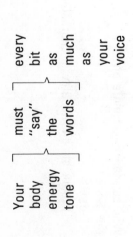

Your		every
body	must	bit
energy }	"say" }	as
tone	the	much
	words	as
		your
		voice

Equally as important: everyone on stage
must be alert
   responsive
   ready to change from one situation to another
     involve himself totally in each new situation.

No matter how comical some of these scenes will prove to be,
play them in dead earnest. The comedy will come from doing the
absurd act with as much earnestness as you would muster
were you involved in one of Hamlet's soul-searching soliloquies.

Don't comment
Don't indicate.

DO.

Carrythrough

All your life you should study the work of performers in movies and plays and television. View them as if they were an extra, fun, and rewarding classroom devised especially for you to learn more about the art of acting.

Think about it.
Who can teach you more about comedy than Charlie Chaplin
the Marx Brothers
Laurel and Hardy
W. C. Fields
Lucille Ball
Carol Burnett?

Who can teach you more about
the detail
depth
irreducible individuality of characterization than Marlon Brando
George C. Scott
Maggie Smith
Lee Grant?

Take advantage of these artists and their work.
They can teach you much if you take the time

and

effort

to

learn.

In the style of _____

Choose a scene.

Do it in the style of

a color: mauve
red
blue
silver
white
black

an actor: Al Pacino
Rod Steiger
James Dean
Hedy Lamarr

a food: pizza
oatmeal
popcorn
oil

a geographical region: Texas
India
Mississippi
Sweden

a playwright: Brecht
Shakespeare
Beckett
Pirandello

a painting: a Miro
Degas
Toulouse-Lautrec
Magritte

an art form: a ballet
comic book
opera

a sport: basketball
        chess
        tennis

Carrythrough

As with movies so with all these forms, foods, and faces,
experience them
analyze them
research them.

Use your imagination and skill to assimilate them and
      master them so you can
      use them as stylistic models.

Style from props

Two to four actors are given three props and nothing else.
Let characterization and content and style of the scene
evolve from using the three props:

    fan / fencing swords / mirror

    letter / glass / sweater

dress / shoes / pumpkin

couch / tube of lipstick / loose change

bologna / beer / cards

book / spyglass / hat

curtain / needle / thread

piano / tap shoes / cigarette

_____

Carrythrough

Make certain you can do everything that the property asks.
Master whatever you cannot do: tap dancing
            fencing
             rolls and falls
              and so on
               and on

Masks

Buy, rent, borrow, or, best of all, make a mask.

Put it on.

Let it work on you.

You and the mask play a scene.

Possible situations:

person waving final goodbye to loved one

person painting his masterpiece on a canvas

person preparing himself to be
the best-dressed person at the ball

When wearing a mask it is not possible to use your eyes and face to convey emotion. A mask acts as a kind of projector, throwing focus on your body. For your body to project all the emotion typically projected by both face and body, you must feel the emotion strongly and project it in clear, clean, large movements.

If you are really "wearing" the mask
you will have the same "face" as the mask.

Masks ask the actor to take the small psychological gesture and make it large and theatrical, all the while never forsaking but increasing its psychological truth.

Movement from numbers or letters

Move in space.

Base your floor pattern
and/or torso movement
arm movement
finger movement on a number or letter form: the figure 8

0
4
7
2

the letter z
b
p
q
m

Change the space/Change the form

Prepare an improvisatory scene on a proscenium stage.
Do the same scene

in the round
in a small room
in a large room
outdoors

as if it were being televised (or
actually video tape it if you can)
as if it were in Madison Square Garden.

COMIC IMPROVISATIONS

Using your sense of the absurd,
but treating it seriously,
improvise situations like the following:

a group of pessimists together at an optimists' convention

a scene based on a review of a play

____ Prepare the scene as the reviewer saw it.
____ Bring nothing to the scene
other than what the reviewer said was there.

a scene of discovery

Adele Davis is discovered to be
a health food devotee.

a scene of conflict

In Horn & Hardart
there are five automats and fifteen people.
Everyone is in a rush and hungry.
All have change
but no one has the exact change.

a social gathering commemorating the death of the potato chip
rancid grape award
inmate
demonstrator
pervert   } of the year award
authoritarian
breast feeder

a classroom or social gathering of high school types: jock
cheerleader
lovesick girl
with-it boy
bookworm
class president
class treasurer
girl friend of
football captain
violin player

a party consisting of authority figures,
each trying to assert h$^{er}_{is}$ authority: medical doctor
high school principal
college president
Secretary of State
editor of the *Detroit Express*
president of General Motors

Study the types you are going to enact
(as well as using your own memory).

Don't condescend to them.
Become them, and
play their comic action seriously.

Carrythrough

Observe comic types of people in the real world off stage.

Charlie Chaplin would follow a person around for weeks observing h$^{er}_{is}$ every move, h$^{er}_{is}$ every action and reaction, until he felt he could truly represent the person on stage.

You need to work at least as hard as Chaplin in order to transform yourself to character.

CARRYTHROUGH

When you are working on a scene for class or a play,
use and freely adapt any of these improvisations
(and invent some of your own).

In warm-ups,
to get everyone energizing themselves
       coordinating their voices and bodies
            having a good time doing it

try some of the games.

To develop an ensemble spirit
use any of the trust improvisations.

To get added insights or
a fresh view of the scene and your character:

    Play the scene focusing on environmental factors
                    what's happening off stage.

    Improvise what happened before the scene began
                    you think will happen after it ends.

Work on the scene's or your character's rhythm:
use music
    clapped rhythms
    an internal character rhythm.

Figure out and play your character's dynamic in the scene:
do you get happier
    sadder
    calmer while everyone else gets more excited
        frustrated
        silly?

Decide what your character's secret aversion and attraction
is for everyone else in the scene.
Play the scene focusing on the aversion or attraction.

Do the scene as if you were animals
    objects
    naked
    foods
    colors
    instruments.

Dream your characters dreams.

Fantasize his/her daydreams.

302

Do any of these improvisations

adapting them however you choose

to discover and play

the real
spontaneous life

of your character and the play.

10. TECHNIQUE

Technique is such a loaded term,
so often used and misused, that one all but avoids mentioning it.
Yet both a theoretical and practical understanding are absolutely essential
to any actor who is serious about plying his trade.

Hence, however problematical, polemical, and perverse this term,
let us deal with it head on.
Let's clear away its chaff
since its wheat is so worth the saving.

Why is the term "technique" so problematical?

One reason is that
it has frequently been used in arguments to polarize actors.
On the one hand, say the polarizers,
are actors who are true to themselves and the moment
but unable to move well or talk loudly;
they *are not* technique actors.
On the other hand are actors who are unfeeling
but physically and vocally skillful;
they *are* technique actors.

The polarizers go on
to urge actors to excell in *either* technique *or* truth.
The underlying assumption of this argument is that
it is impossible for an actor to be both:
either s/he can feel
or s/he can talk and move
but never both at the same time and in the same place.

This argument is as fatuous as it is dangerous.

Actors must be able both to feel and
                    to project their feeling in sound and movement.

Otherwise they are not actors;
they are half actors.
Their parallel is a singer who has a good voice but is tone deaf or
a dancer who admires turns, twists, and leaps but
is too weak-kneed to execute them himself.
The tone-deaf singer and the weak-kneed dancer are useless to their
    professions;
so are the actor who mumbles and stumbles truthfully
and the one who skillfully communicates nothing.

What is called for is an actor who is a whole performer,
one who believes what s/he is doing
        is able to communicate that belief in an action
                on a stage
                        to an audience.

Technique is a way of accomplishing that communication.
It is nothing more.
It is nothing less.

Think of it this way:
Acting is an expression that depends on equal measures of pretense and truth.

P   In plays actors pretend they are other people than they are;
and those people they are pretending to be are, by turns, agile

R   lissome
                                                                 weak
                                                                 strong
E   violent

T   singer
                                                                 dancer
                                                                 acrobat
E   rich wo/man
                                                                 poor wo/man
                                                                 beggar wo/man
                                                                 thief.

N   Actors pretend they are with someone else
                            (than they are with)
                        somewhere else
S   (than they are)
                    living a series of spontaneous events
                            (that they have already rehearsed
E   and whose end they know).

T Actors must take this elaborate web of pretense,

R

U believe in it,

T

H and truthfully communicate the reality of that belief to the audience.

Technique gives actors the necessary physical, vocal, and psychological tools
to accomplish that communication:

Technique is an actor's passport to freedom.

It has three parts,
each and every one of which must be understood and mastered
before an actor is *free* to perform:

Technique of psychology

An actor learns to activate and control his own intelligence

awareness

feeling states

attitudes

imagination

actions

reactions.

Technique of creation

An actor learns how to feel
    understand
    become character alone
        with others
        with a director.

Technique of craft

An actor trains h^{er}mself
and is trained by others
to have such physical and vocal control that
s/he can communicate the character s/he has created
    the action of the play   to the audience.

The bulk of this book has been devoted to the psychological
and creative work of the actor. Craft has been discussed but it
should be treated in greater, more practical detail.

TECHNIQUE FOR DEVELOPING YOUR BODY

Sports

Get with other people.
Play certain competitive sports

that, rather than isometric (muscle building),
are isotonic (stretching): tennis
                                volleyball
                                badminton
                                touch football
                                bowling

or sport by yourself: ice skate
                        roller skate
                        jog
                        bicycle
                        swim.

Sports are marvelous for your acting body and spirit. When you
play them—however well or poorly—not only do they divert and
relax you but they

    stretch you

    tone you up

    help you develop a flexible
                        agile
                        responsive body

        help you coordinate small and large body actions and breathing

involve complete rhythmic actions: preparation
action
carrythrough
response

develop and stretch your energy resources

teach you to react quickly

involve predetermination of object and
subsequent directing of thought and energy toward achieving that object.

Games

Play poker
bridge
chess
monopoly
scrabble.

These games are not only fun,
they are useful for acting in that they teach you to

work in units

go for objectives

play intentions as you try to psych out the other player(s)

observe other people's intentions, text, and subtext
as they try to psych you out.

Notice how adherence to form and rules reveals the character
and personality of the players.

Tasks

Sit in the lotus position
while you are reading or listening to a lecture.

Exercise while you are listening to the news.

Breathe deeply while you are walking to school or wherever.
Breathe in through the nose
out through the mouth to a count of eight.

While you are doing household chores
tune into and discover your body:

What is my relationship to gravity?
Where does my muscle strength have to be
When I am scrubbing a sink
    making a bed
      carrying out garbage
        hammering a nail
          sawing a board
            reaching up to clean or get something from a cupboard?

Learn how to use the muscles that are called for and only those
muscles. In this way, as you learn about your body you also learn to
do tasks as efficiently as possible—an efficiency that will stand you
in good stead not only in maintaining the house but also in acting on
stage.

Dance

Modern dance is of extraordinary use to the actor.
It realizes an idea, a reaction, an impulse through movement
stresses freedom and stretch and flexible response
stresses the mind as well as the body
teaches the actor to put words and ideas in his/her body
    live them through movement.

Classical ballet is of very limited value to the actor principally because its vocabulary and expression are structural and nonorganic, not tied to or proceeding from impulse. This is not to deny that it may be a useful adjunct in training—particularly in mastering certain styles of acting; but it does not provide the broad or adaptable movement base for the actor that modern dance can.

Also take classes in tap dancing
folk dancing
tumbling
fencing
circus technique: juggling, using a trampoline, etc.
karate
judo.

Postscript

Ballroom dancing
can be as good for your acting
as it is fun for your real self.

It involves sharing of moods
relies on subtle body and mental communication
encourages you to respond to the environment around you
                    to clothing
                    to the touch
                         mood
                         rhythm of another.

TECHNIQUE FOR DEVELOPING YOUR VOICE

Take singing lessons.

Take voice development lessons.

Sing in the shower
    walking down the street
    to your radio or stereo
then sing what you just sang an octave above
                                        below.

Discover pitches outside: subway
                          bus
                          elevators
                          fluorescent lights
                          people talking to you.

Hum these pitches as you listen to them and activate your resonators.

Call to people at a distance.
If there is no one there imagine somebody.

Learn to play the recorder; it trains your ear for pitch
is good for breath control
is fun to play.

Learn to play other musical instruments as well.

Read aloud for yourself
the blind
the long living
children
anybody.

Go someplace where no one else is.
SCREAM.
You can always use a good scream in most plays and
you can get rid of frustration at the same time.

All these suggestions for developing your body and voice are
made with the clear knowledge that, no matter how determined
you are in your preparation, there will never be a time when you
have total mastery of all the physical and vocal skills that might
be demanded of you.

317

No actor can be expected to know and be ready to perform all things at all times. But all actors can be expected to have a flexible and ready instrument.

Follow these suggestions for developing your body and voice and you will have such a tuned and toned instrument.

TECHNIQUE FOR ENTERING THE ACTION

There is always a surge of energy
before you have to perform in front of a group,
whether in a classroom or before an opening-night audience
as well as any and all points between these two extremes.
Butterflies swoop around.
The adrenalin rises.

Learn to use that energy rather than letting it use you.

Make-up

Applying make-up is an important skill to master, and the process can be just as—even more—important than the result. That half-hour to hour you use to make yourself up is a period of time given over to putting yourself in a state of physical and psychological readiness for acting the role. You have time to relax and shed the day's other worries. You have time to think through knotty bits of business or dialogue.

And at the same time, you are assuming the external mien of your character. Your careful, deliberate choices of color, shade, and lining reveal and help you transform to character.

Learn to watch and enjoy your character coming to life
brush stroke by brush stroke
under your hand and
before your eyes.

Warm-ups

Before you go on stage
get your body and voice loose
         warm
           ready.

Say the following phrase six times, faster each time:

    "The tip of the tongue
    the lips and the teeth."

Make circles with your arms, shoulders, neck.

Throw away your arms, your legs, your torso.

319

Do rag-doll jumps.

Drop at your waist with legs bent.
Spring up and out as though you were shooting a basketball.

___ Develop your own set of exercises. Always pay particular
___ attention to loosening the voice and the upper body: you can
___ work with a certain tension in your lower body, but tension in
___ your upper body affects your projection and can hurt you.

When you have made yourself ready to enter the action
and then do so you will undoubtedly experience a sudden
surge of energy flooding through you. In those first few
adrenalin-filled moments of being on stage, *use* your
excess energy rather than letting it overpower you:

  Use a slightly bigger voice than necessary.

  Use a bigger gesture.

  Cross the stage with a little more force.

  Concentrate harder on your intentions.

When you have gotten safely beyond those critical moments
you will be able to settle in and play the play.

TECHNIQUE OF PLAYING THE SPACE

The technique of playing the space is merely introduced here, because it reaches its full development only in performance before a live audience. Only then are all the elements of living theatre space presented.

Following are a few generalized rubrics for different kinds of playing areas.

Thrust and arena stages

Proscenium stages

Sensitize your body in all directions; there is always someone looking at your back.

Heighten the sensitivity in the part of the body facing the audience. Use no less energy here than on the thrust stage, but focus it more toward the part of the body exposed to the audience.

Radiate performance energy in circles in all directions around your body and the bodies of the actors you're working with, concentrically toward the audience.

Focus your energy in a linear direction toward other actors and the audience.

Because your back frequently faces the audience, your vocal technique is unusually important. Develop it so that your voice can express to people who can't see your face as much as you express to people who can.

Because you are prompted to move in curves, in diagonals, and in a compact space, moving in depth more than in horizontals, make your crosses shorter in thrust.

No less vocal effectiveness is required when you perform on a proscenium stage. But because you frequently face the audience or are at least no more than half turned away, relax your projection a bit.

Because you are moving in linear directions, make bigger, longer crosses and motivate them more intensely.

TECHNIQUE OF GIVING THE FOCUS

On all stages, develop an awareness of how to give and take focus.

Know what is happening in the action at each moment
    how the action is being developed
    who is most important
    who has secondary importance.

Through your expressive and meaningful use of body and voice give and take the focus necessary to carry the action forward.

CARRYTHROUGH

This chapter has suggested numerous ways to carry your development of craft in your workaday life. Sports, cleaning house, games, dancing, singing to the radio have all been advanced as ways you can improve your craft as you live your life.

Undoubtedly there are other things each of you does in your life that can be used to develop your acting craft.

Decide what they are.

Use them.

11. Rules of the Game

Albert Camus adhered to no religious or philosophical school,
yet he was an acknowledged ethical leader of the twentieth century.

Asked to reveal the inspiration of his ethical system
Camus replied it was sports,
which asks of its players
loyal obedience to rules of the game,
jointly defined and freely accepted.

That request suggested a code of behavior
sufficient to any life situation.
It is certainly sufficient
to the communal event of the theatre.

Over the centuries of theatre's life
some "rules of the game" have evolved.
The degree to which the members of each new theatre community
jointly modify these rules to their particular needs
and then freely accept them
is the degree to which they make themselves
responsive and responsible
to their community.

The rules of the theatre game are not moralistic or restrictive.
They are pragmatic,
formulated for the sole purpose of
making the cooperative venture of theatre
a workable, creative reality.

For only within limits proscribed by rules
can each person working in the theatre find his own freedom
to create and produce.

FREEDOM WITHIN LIMITS
is the keynote of creativity in the theatre.

Without such rules of the game

without such freedom within limits

chaos results.

Be healthy.

No matter how prepared
talented
cooperative an actor you are,
it does no one any good if you are home sick in bed
while the play rehearses and performs.

A sick, tired body cannot possibly meet
the extraordinary physical and emotional demands of theatre.

So get yourself in shape
and stay in shape.

Even in his sixties Laurence Olivier still
goes to the gym twice a week to keep fit.

In your teens and twenties
(and thirties and forties)
you should work out every day.

Exercise should be part of your life-art routine.

When you wake up in the morning or
before you go to bed at night
or at any time in between,
set aside time to tune up and tone up your body.

Do sit-ups
     push-ups
          bicycles.
     Stand on your shoulders.
Jog.
Bend and stretch.
Chin yourself.
Do deep-breathing exercises.

Be creative—
invent your own exercises.

Make a daily routine of them.

Stick to your routine.

Eat right.

Get sufficient protein
    fresh fruits
      vegetables
       vitamins
       minerals.

If you are in doubt about nutritional
requirements for a healthy body,
go to the library and
get a book on nutrition.
You cannot afford not to know
what foods to eat to keep you healthy.

Being low on funds is no excuse
for not eating right.

    Powdered skim milk
    eggs
    cottage cheese
    are inexpensive complete protein foods
    that are cheaper than a high-fat, chemical hot dog or
        sugar-and-spiced cold cuts.

Brewer's yeast is inexpensive and
has B vitamins,
plus protein and minerals.

Other good cheap foods: yogurt
soybeans
lentils
nuts
seeds
wheat germ

The burgeoning number of food coops around the country
allow you to get fresh fruits
vegetables
whole grain cereals and breads
at a fraction of the cost you pay for them at supermarkets.

If there is no coop around you get together with some people
and start one yourself. Look at the People's Yellow Pages for
advice.

So eat well and

develop a series of exercises

to keep yourself ready for

the physically and emotionally demanding event of theatre.

Be on time.

Short of an emergency
no excuse justifies
one person wasting the time and energy of others.

Whether for a rehearsal between two people
working on a classroom exercise
or for an opening-night call,
be on time.

That does not mean that you arrive at 7:00
for a 7:00 call.

It means that you arrive in sufficient time to take off your coat
    go to the bathroom
    drink your tiger's milk and
    be ready to begin work at 7:00.

Forget your problems.

Theatre is a community event:
the welfare of the community must be *protected* and *promoted*
if theatre is to happen.

331

Don't depress the spirit of the community.

If you arrive at rehearsal tired
               unhappy in love
               sick in body or soul
               pressed for time
               out of sorts

   forget it for the time being.

Rather than being preciously concerned about yourself
(and asking others to be likewise concerned),
focus your attention on the play and the players.
After all, that's why all of you are there.

Think of it this way:

Listening to someone else complain
doesn't put you in a creative and productive mood.

Neither does listening to your problems inspire others.

  A game you might play
  if someone else is depressed:
  See what you can do in fifteen minutes
  to raise his spirit.

Have zest and energy for the work to be done.

Theatre work is not something to be got over as quickly as possible. It is a privilege and a joy.

Dont arrive at rehearsal only to watch the clock till you leave.

Be ready and wanting to work.

Can you imagine Picasso painting in a lackluster way, watching the clock, eagerly anticipating the hour when he can escape his painting and start to live?
Of course not.
For Picasso his work was the most vital part of his life.
So must yours be.

If you don't enjoy the work of the theatre— and there is *lots* of it— get out.
Find work you will enjoy.

Learn to take part in constructive, nonthreatening critical dialogue.

While there are certain exclusively personal problems that you should avoid discussing in rehearsal because they have nothing to do with the group endeavor, there are matters of community concern that must be discussed. Learning to discuss these matters in a helpful way is an art in itself.

When you offer criticism,
suggest rather than command.

If you say to someone
"I wonder if this might work"
and then carefully spell out your plan of action,
the recipient of your advice will probably not get upset.
You haven't threatened h~im~.

But if you say to someone
"That's the wrong way. Do it this way."
you make h~im~ wrong,
put h~im~ on the defensive,
and effectively close the door of communication.

In art, there are no rights and wrongs
goods and bads.
These terms are absolutes that belong more properly to theology than theatre.
In theatre things are more human
and therefore more relative.
So offer your criticism in a spirit
of camaraderie and relativity.

Likewise
when someone criticizes you,
be it the director
    a fellow actor
        the costume designer or
            whoever,
understand that (however much it may hurt you)
the criticism is usually not meant to destroy you.

It is meant to help you.

Look at criticism as a free gift
that can make you better if it is perceptive
and can really do you no harm if it is not.

If, however,
the criticism is offered in a hostile way,
you have every right,
indeed the obligation,
to take the person aside
after—*not during*—rehearsal
and discuss his[er] hostility.
You can explain in a helpful way that
his[er] criticism did not offend you
but the manner of criticism did.
In this way both of you can profit from the mistake,

as both of you learn how to contribute better to one another's growth.

Group ideas should develop with the same spirit of camaraderie give and take relativity.

If a fellow actor
suggests a way to do something in a scene and you then think of another way,
don't say "No!" to h$_{is}^{er}$ suggestion.
Say instead something like,
"That might work, or how about this?"
and offer your suggestion.

In this way you feed off one suggestion,
advance another, and
make it possible for the next person to advance h$_{is}^{ers}$,
until you creatively and cooperatively
arrive at the best solution.

Do your private work.

When you get an insight into your character or your action from yourself, a fellow actor, or the director,
go home after rehearsal and
make it your own.

Justify it.
Practice it until it is yours.
Then the next night you will be ready to learn more.

Don't trust
that you will remember everything you learned in rehearsal.

Write down any notes the director gives you
and jot down any other worthwhile advice or insight.
Then go home and that night or the next day
reread the script and work on those notes.

The next night you won't have to waste valuable group time
learning what has previously been given you.
You will be ready to go on
and learn more things.

Let your character evolve.

Don't arrive at rehearsals in a state of anxiety about
whether or not you are going to be "good" in the role.

You should not expect to have a full-blown character
the first week or two of rehearsal and then
worry yourself sick if you don't have it.
Usually a play is given four to six weeks of rehearsal,

and this is for a good reason:
it takes that long for everything to happen,
for characters to evolve and for the play to come together.

Do each day's private work as well as you can.

Do each night's public rehearsal work as well as you can.

Stay free and easy during rehearsal.

Experiment.
Try this.
If it doesn't work discard it.
Try something else.

Take suggestions.
Work your hardest on them.

Offer suggestions.

Let things happen.

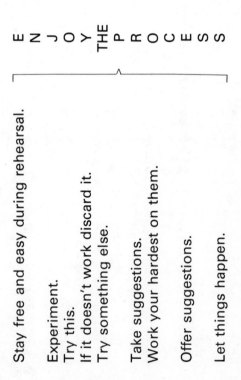

ENJOY THE PROCESS

Trust that in the course of your work
the character will grow and find his/her proper life.

Dont play precious.

Ironic though it may seem,
theatre is no place for the person of great vanity.

In most theatre you will have to scream
     cry
     tumble
     crawl.

You will get bruised
     roughed up
     dirty
     tired.

You will alternately be called upon to roll on the floor
     get a pie in the face
     hang by your knees from a scaffolding
     tumble downstairs
     take a pratfall.

If in the course of rehearsal someone accidently hurts you in some way,
don't tremble, get angry, scream, cry, or faint.
In any production accidents are bound to happen.
Unless you have a mad wo/man in the crowd,
no one means to hurt you.

If you react unduly to a fellow actor's accidentally hurting you,
you risk making him so nervous that
s/he will be afraid to do anything around you.
If other actors treat you like a rare hothouse plant
it is you who will suffer in rehearsal and performance.

In this same pell-mell spirit
don't be afraid of getting your hands
                face
                body
                feet   dirty.

In the theatre you are your own stunt man.
If you are too fragile to endure some dirt
           a lump
           a bump
           a blow

theatre is probably not the place for you.

Respect the worth of others.

Each of the many artists and artisans in the theatre
has his task to perform in the theatre community.

box office personnel
director
actors
scene/costume/property/lighting designers
scene/costume/property/lighting technicians
playwright
ushers
producer

Not one of these people is there to serve you.

All of you together
are there to serve the *play*
and, ultimately, the *audience.*

Humility not humiliation.

Don't condescend to anyone else in the theatre
any more than you would permit anyone else condescend to you.

As an actor you have responsibilities
but you also have rights.
Exercise both.

Don't decide that a more experienced actor
or one with a larger role
or a bigger name
or the playwright or the director

342

has all the answers and
yours is not to reason why,
yours is but to agree and sigh.
You too are a creator.
You too can question how things are done
and make suggestions about the way they should be done.

A director worth h$^{er}_{is}$ salt knows how to feed off
the suggestions of the actors,
just as an actor worth h$^{er}_{is}$ salt knows how to feed off
suggestions of the director.

There are no gods in the theatre,

only a group of dedicated, creative people
working together toward a common goal:

doing a play for an audience.

Within limits find your freedom.
Commit yourself.
Be engaged.
Go all the way with what you do.
WORK.

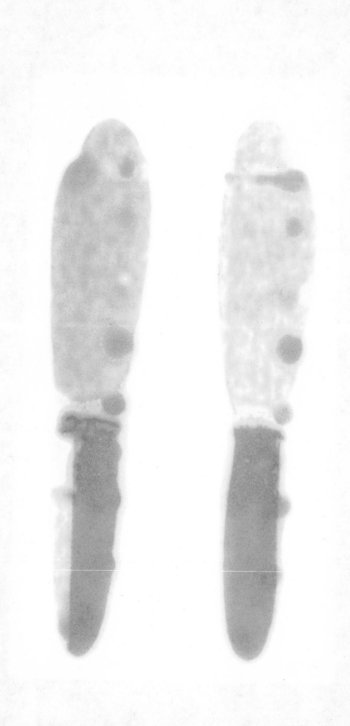